Hal Leonard GUITAR METHOD
by Will Schmid

BOOK 1

Dr. Will Schmid is the author of the best selling *Hal Leonard Guitar Method* (in nine languages) and over forty books for guitar and banjo, cassettes, CDs, and a video tape for Hal Leonard Publishing. In addition to his own writing, Will has served as editor of a wide variety of Hal Leonard's methods and guitar publications. He is professor of music at the University of Wisconsin–Milwaukee where he chairs the Guitar Performance Program. He holds a B.A. from Luther College and a Ph.D. from the Eastman School of Music. He has given workshops throughout the United States and in Australia, Canada and Europe. From 1994-96 Dr. Schmid served as president of the 63,000-member Music Educators National Conference (MENC) and as a founder of the MENC/GAMA Guitar Task Force. Will performs as a finger-style and flat-pick guitarist in a singing duo with his wife Ann, autoharpist and director of the nationally known Stringalong Workshops.

CONTENTS

Foreword..2
Your Guitar...2
Tuning 3
Playing Position 4
Musical Symbols 5
Notes on the First String 6
Notes on the Second String............................8
   ODE TO JOY..10
   ROUND 10
Notes on the Third String...............................10
   YANKEE DOODLE 12
   THE BELLS (Duet).....................................12
   AU CLAIR DE LA LUNE (Duet) 13
   AURA LEE..14
   HE'S A JOLLY GOOD FELLOW 14
3-String Chords—C, G, G7.............................15
Guitar Solos 16
   MARIANNE...16
   DOWN IN THE VALLEY 16
Notes on the Fourth String 17
   THE RIDDLE SONG 18
The D7 Chord...19
   12-BAR BLUES-ROCK..............................19
   WORRIED MAN BLUES 20
   AMAZING GRACE......................................20
   WHEN THE SAINTS GO MARCHING IN.............21
   THE GYPSY GUITAR.................................21
Notes on the Fifth String 22
   BLUES BASS..22
   THE VOLGA BOATMAN............................23
   GREENSLEEVES 23
Notes on the Sixth String 24
   JOHNNY HAS GONE FOR A SOLDIER...................25
   BASS ROCK 25

Half and Whole Steps 26
F-sharp 26
   LONDONDERRY AIR...............................26
Key Signatures 27
   SHENANDOAH (Duet)...............................27
Rests...28
   ROCK 'N' REST 29
   JACK STUART 29
The Full C, G and G7 Chords 30
   WILL THE CIRCLE BE UNBROKEN.....32
   CORINNA...32
   IRISH TUNE..33
The Bass Note/Strum 33
Eighth Notes...34
   DRUNKEN SAILOR...................................35
   FRERE JACQUES.......................................35
   KOOKABURRA...35
   BOOGIE BASS...36
   3-PART ROUND..36
The E Minor Chord 37
   HEY, HO, NOBODY HOME.......................37
   SHALOM CHAVERIM................................37
   MOLLY MALONE..38
More Advanced Strums......................................39
   SIMPLE GIFTS..40
Bass-Melody Solos...42
   ROW, ROW, ROW YOUR BOAT................42
   WORRIED MAN BLUES 42
   WHEN THE SAINTS GO MARCHING IN.............43
New Note - C#...43
   MINUET IN G (Duet).................................44
   GUITAR ENSEMBLE.................................46
Chord Chart..47

HAL•LEONARD® CORPORATION

7777 W. BLUEMOUND RD. P.O. BOX 13819 MILWAUKEE, WI 53213

FOREWORD

Since the first edition of this method was published in 1977, I have talked with thousands of guitar teachers about how the method worked for them. This feedback has been essential in building supplements to the method and a catalog with real integrity. When I decided to revise Book 1, I sent out a survey to a panel of leading guitar teachers, who answered a series of questions and marked up the book. In your hands is the fruit of our labors, and a further reason why the Hal Leonard Guitar Method (published in 8 languages) will gain wider acceptance by teachers and students. Thanks to Kirk Likes, Larry Beekman, Jim Skinger, Harold Hooper, Jim Cooney, John Campbell, George Widiger, Mike Alwin, John Dragonetti, Tony Collova, Gary Wolk and Debi Kossoris.

Will Schmid

YOUR GUITAR

This book is designed for use with any type of guitar — acoustic steel-string, nylon-string classic or electric. Any of these guitars can be adapted to use in a wide variety of styles of music.

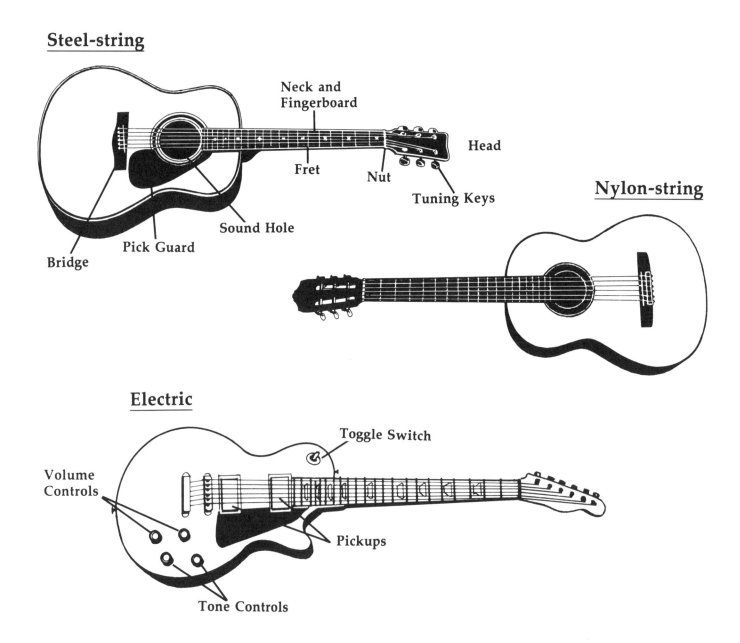

Steel-string

Neck and Fingerboard

Head

Fret

Nut

Tuning Keys

Sound Hole

Pick Guard

Bridge

Nylon-string

Electric

Toggle Switch

Volume Controls

Pickups

Tone Controls

TUNING (Indicates Audio Track Number)

Tuning to a Piano

When you are tuning your guitar, you will adjust the pitch (highness or lowness of sound) of each string by turning the corresponding tuning key. Tightening a string raises the pitch and loosening it lowers the pitch.

The strings are numbered 1 through 6 beginning with the thinnest string, the one closest to your knee. Tune each string in sequence beginning with the **sixth** string, by playing the correct key on the piano (see diagram) and slowly turning the tuning key until the sound of the string matches the sound of the piano.

Tuning with an Electronic Guitar Tuner

An electronic tuner "reads" the pitch of a sound and tells you whether or not the pitch is correct. Until your ear is well trained in hearing pitches, this can be a much more accurate way to tune. There are many different types of tuners available, and each one will come with more detailed instructions for its use.

1—E
2—B
3—G
4—D
5—A
6—E

TUNING KEYS

Keyboard

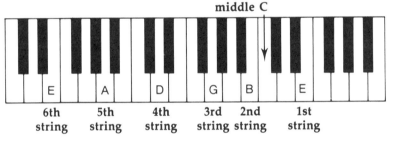

middle C

| 6th string | 5th string | 4th string | 3rd string | 2nd string | 1st string |

E A D G B E

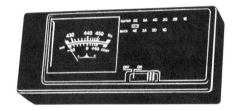

Relative Tuning

To check or correct your tuning when no pitch source is available, follow these steps:

• Assume that the sixth string is tuned correctly to E.

• Press the sixth string at the 5th fret. This is the pitch A to which you tune your open fifth string. Play the depressed sixth string and the fifth string with your thumb. When the two sounds match, you are in tune.

• Press the fifth string at the 5th fret and tune the open fourth string to it. Follow the same procedure that you did on the fifth and sixth strings.

• Press the fourth string at the 5th fret and tune the open third string to it.

• To tune the second string, press the third string at the 4th fret and tune the open second string to it.

• Press the second string at the 5th fret and tune the first string to it.

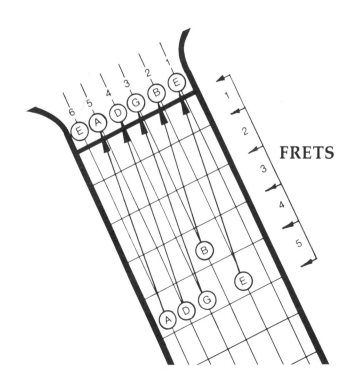

FRETS

PLAYING POSITION

There are several ways to hold the guitar comfortably. On the left is a typical seated position, and on the right is the standing position. Observe the following general guidelines in forming your playing posture:

- Position your body, arms and legs in such a way that you **avoid tension.**

- If you feel tension creeping into your playing, you probably need to reassess your position.

- Tilt the neck upwards—never down.

- Keep the body of the guitar as vertical as possible. Avoid slanting the top of the guitar so that you can see better. Balance your weight evenly from left to right. Sit straight (but not rigid).

Left-hand fingers are numbered 1 through 4. (Pianists: Note that the thumb is not number 1.) Place the thumb in back of the neck roughly opposite the 2nd finger as shown below. Avoid gripping the neck like a baseball bat with the palm touching the back of the neck.

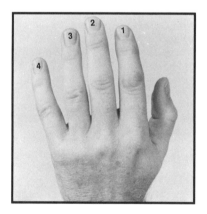

These photos show the position for holding a pick and the right-hand position in relationship to the strings. Strive for finger efficiency and relaxation in your playing.

MUSICAL SYMBOLS

Music is written in **notes** on a **staff.** The staff has five lines and four spaces between the lines. Where a note is written on the staff determines its **pitch** (highness or lowness). At the beginning of the staff is a **clef sign.** Guitar music is written in the treble clef.

Each line and space of the staff has a letter name: The **lines** are, (from bottom to top) E - G - B - D - F (which you can remember as Every Guitarist Begins Doing Fine): The spaces are from bottom to top, F - A - C - E, which spells "Face."

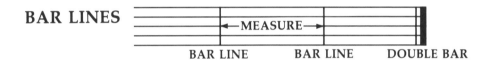

The staff is divided into several parts by bar lines. The space between two bar lines is called a measure. To end a piece of music a double bar is placed on the staff.

Each measure contains a group of beats. Beats are the steady pulse of music. You respond to the pulse or beat when you tap your foot.

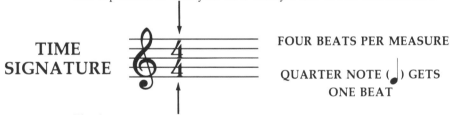

Notes indicate the length (number of counts) of musical sound.

When different kinds of notes are placed on different lines or spaces, you will know the pitch of the note and how long to play the sound.

NOTES ON THE FIRST STRING

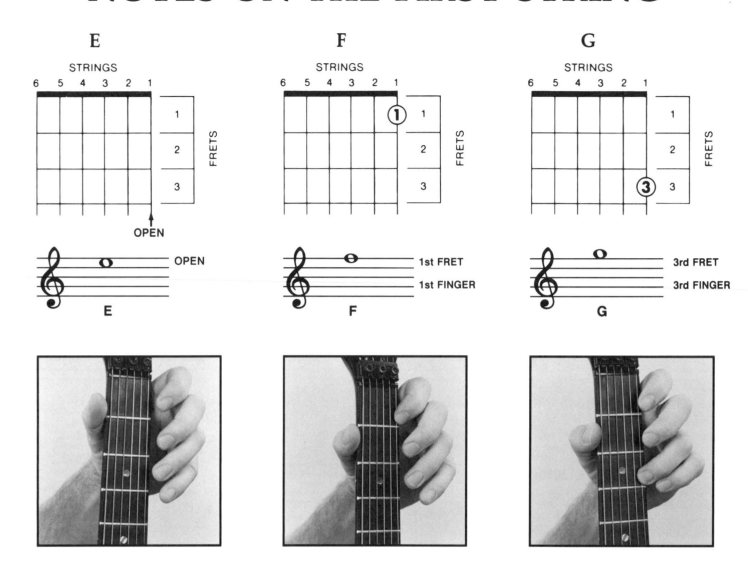

This sign (⊓) tells you to strike the string with a downward motion of the pick.

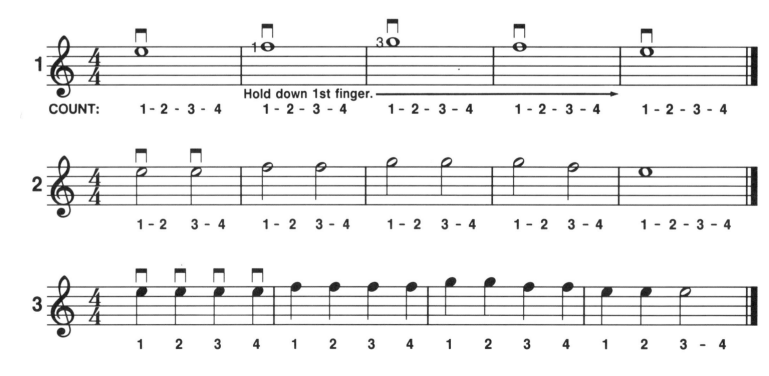

At first practice the exercises slowly and steadily. When you can play them well at a slow speed, gradually increase the tempo (speed).

Touch only the tips of the fingers on the strings.

Keep the left hand fingers arched over the strings.

Some songs are longer than one line. When you reach the end of the first line of music, continue on to the second line without stopping. Grey letters above the staff indicate chords to be played by your teacher. Measure numbers are given at the beginning of each new line of music.

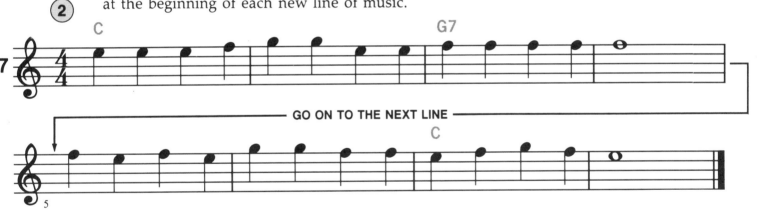

7

NOTES ON THE SECOND STRING

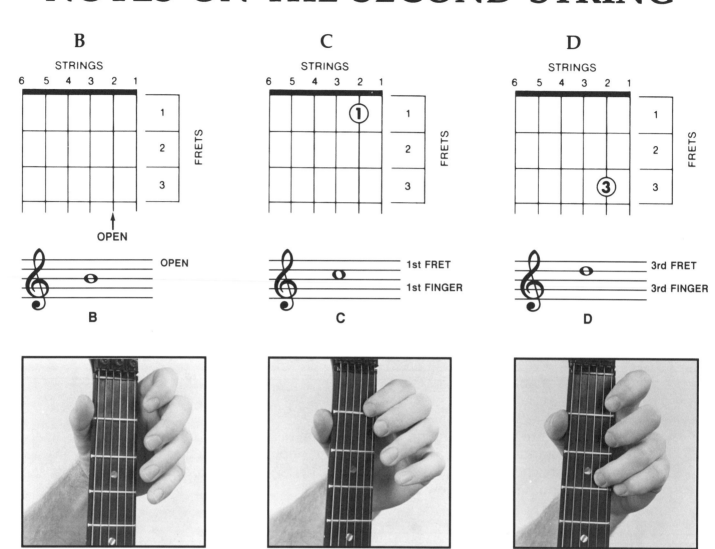

B

STRINGS
6 5 4 3 2 1

FRETS
1
2
3

OPEN

OPEN

B

C

STRINGS
6 5 4 3 2 1

FRETS
1
2
3

1st FRET
1st FINGER

C

D

STRINGS
6 5 4 3 2 1

FRETS
1
2
3

3rd FRET
3rd FINGER

D

9

$\frac{4}{4}$

COUNT: 1 - 2 - 3 - 4   1 - 2 - 3 - 4   1 - 2 - 3 - 4   1 - 2 - 3 - 4   1 - 2 - 3 - 4

Hold down 1st finger.

10

$\frac{4}{4}$

1 - 2   3 - 4   1 - 2   3 - 4   1 - 2   3 - 4   1 - 2   3 - 4   1 - 2 - 3 - 4

11

$\frac{4}{4}$

1   2   3   4   1   2   3   4   1   2   3   4   1   2   3   4   1 - 2 - 3 - 4

Always practice the exercises slowly and steadily at first. After you can play them well at a slower tempo, gradually increase the speed. If some of your notes are fuzzy or unclear, move your left hand finger slightly until you get a clear sound.

Moving From String To String

You have learned six notes now, three on the first string and three on the second string. In the following exercises you will be moving from string to string. As you are playing one note, look ahead to the next and get your fingers in position.

STRING:	②			①		
FINGER:	open	1st	3rd	open	1st	3rd

Practice these songs played on strings 1 and 2. Always begin slowly and then gradually increase the tempo. Gray chord symbols are used throughout the book to indicate that the chords should be played by the instructor.

ODE TO JOY ④ ⑤

Beethoven

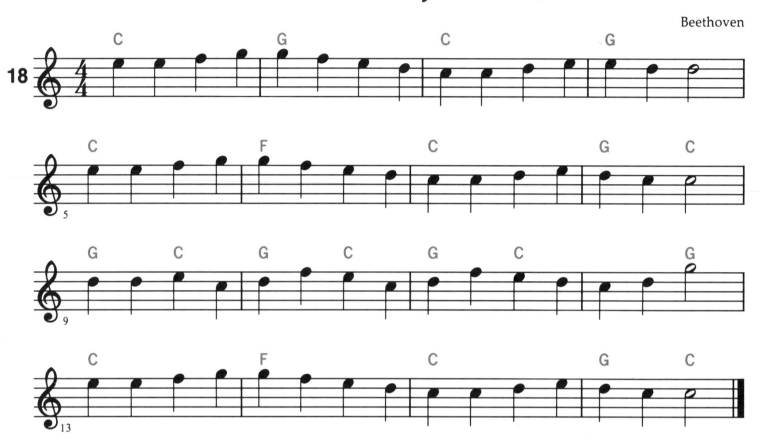

The following piece is a **round** for from 1 to 3 players. Each new player begins when the previous player gets to the asterisk (*). Play it twice through without stopping.

ROUND ⑥

NOTES ON THE THIRD STRING

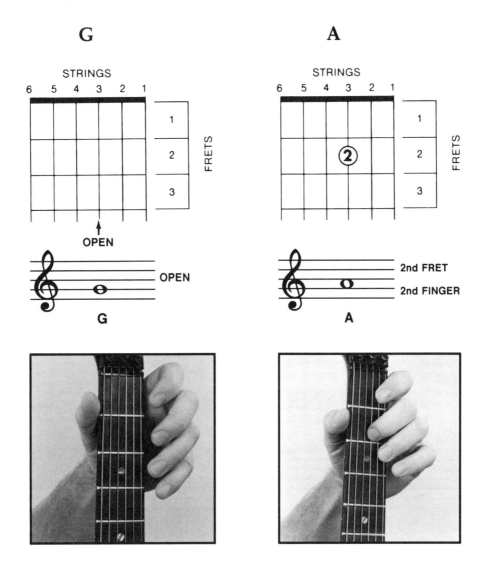

Keep the fingers arched over the strings at all times so they will be in position to finger the next note.

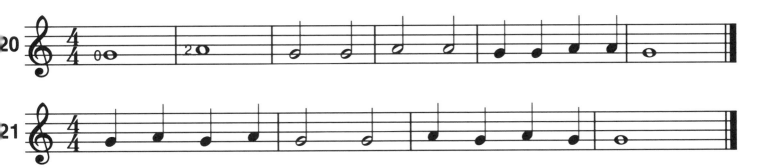

ROCK TRAX - 1

Supplement this book with —

The book/audio pak that teaches you:
• Rhythm guitar • Lead guitar • Solo licks
• Audio features complete rhythm section

— How to Improvise Rock for Beginners —

BOOK/CASSETTE
HL00699167

BOOK/CD
HL00697271

The following exercises and pieces use notes on strings 1, 2 and 3.

22

STRING: ③ — ② — ① — ② — ③

Play for accuracy; then gradually speed up. Use as a finger warm-up.

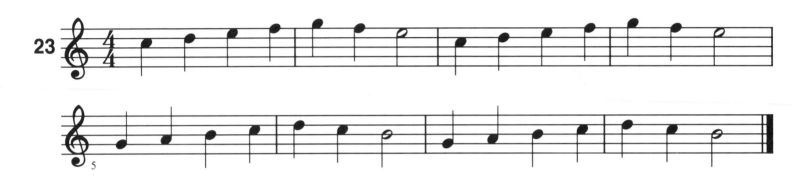

23

YANKEE DOODLE

24

A **duet** is a song that has two parts that can be played together. Practice both parts of the following duet. Ask your instructor or a friend to play the duet with you. If you have a tape recorder, you can record one of the parts and then play a duet with yourself. When you can play both parts, combine them in the optional solo below.

THE BELLS

Duet

Part 1

25

Part 2

Optional Solo

Repeat and Fade

AU CLAIR DE LA LUNE ⑦

France

AURA LEE (8)

Some music has three beats per measure instead of four. This is indicated by the top number of the time signature. The bottom number (4) tells you that the quarter note gets one beat.

A dot after a note increases its value by one-half. In 3/4 time a dotted half note (♩.) gets three beats.

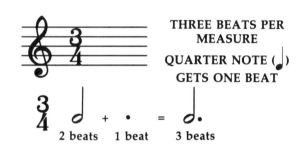

THREE BEATS PER MEASURE

QUARTER NOTE (♩) GETS ONE BEAT

$$\frac{3}{4} \quad \text{♩} + \text{•} = \text{♩•}$$
2 beats　1 beat　3 beats

COUNT:　　1　2　3　1 - 2　3　1　2　3　1 - 2 - 3　1　2 - 3　1 - 2 - 3

HE'S A JOLLY GOOD FELLOW (9)

England

3-STRING CHORDS

A chord is sounded when more than one note or string is played at the same time. To begin you will be playing chords on three strings with only one finger depressed.

Strike strings 3, 2 and 1 with a downward motion. All three strings should sound as one, not separately.

C Chord

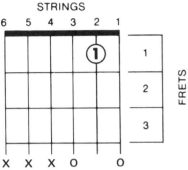

G Chord

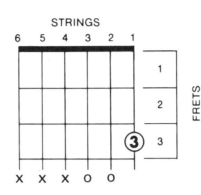

G7 Chord

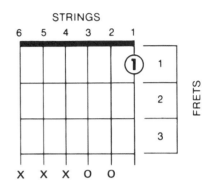

An (o) under a string indicates that the string should be played "OPEN" (not depressed by a finger).

An (x) under a string indicates that the string should not be strummed.

Keep a steady beat, and change chord fingerings quickly.

The chords above are partial chords. If you are ready to learn the full versions of these chords, turn to the **Chord Chart** on page 47.

GUITAR SOLOS

You have been playing either the melody or the chord strums in the previous exercises. Now combine the chords and the melody. First, play through the melodies (the top notes only). When you feel you know the melodies well enough, strum each chord. Finally, combine the melody and the chords. Practice the exercise slowly and steadily and gradually increase the tempo as you progress.

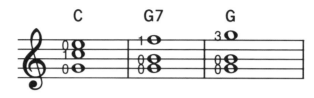

MARIANNE

All day, all night Mar - i - anne,

Down by the sea - side sift - in' sand.

E - ven lit - tle chil - dren love Mar - i - anne,

Down by the sea - side sift - in' sand.

DOWN IN THE VALLEY

Down in the val - ley, val - ley so low,

Hang your head o - ver, Hear the wind blow.

NOTES ON THE FOURTH STRING

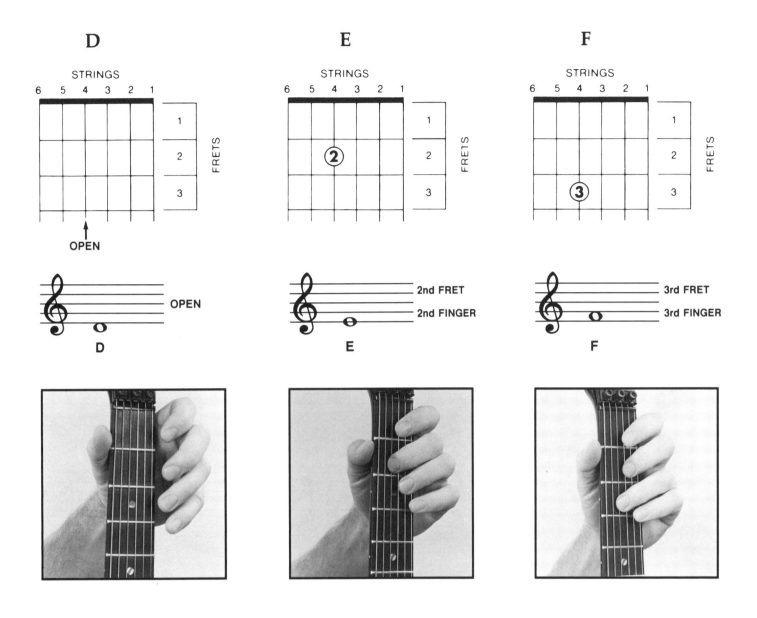

Practice each exercise carefully. Remember to keep your fingers arched over the strings.

Pickup Notes

Music doesn't always begin on beat one. When you begin after beat one, the notes before the first full measure are called pickup notes. the following illustrations show several examples of pickup notes. Count the missing beats out loud before you begin playing.

THE RIDDLE SONG ⑪ ⑫

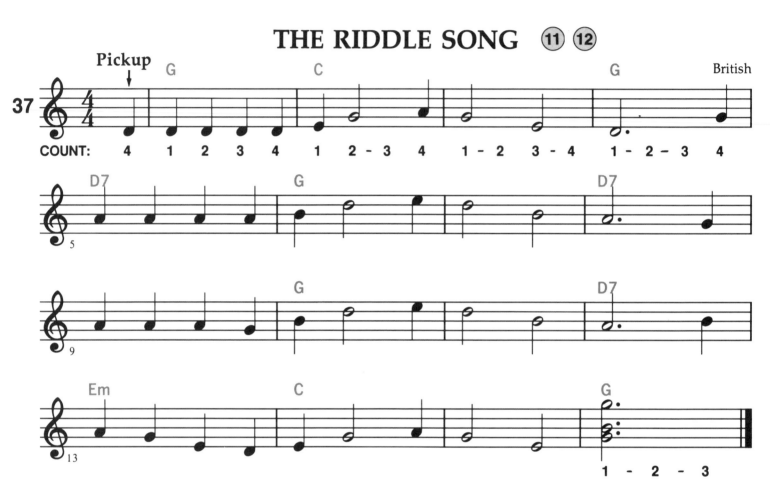

When a song begins with pickup notes, the last measure will be short the exact number of beats used as pickups.

Practice playing both the notes and then the chord strums as a duet with your teacher, a friend or a tape recorder.

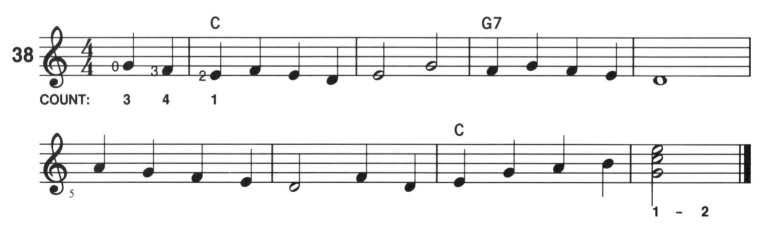

18

THE D7 CHORD

The D7 chord is a triangular formation of the fingers. You can play the full version of this chord right away. Arch your fingers so that the tips touch only one string each. Strum strings 4 through 1 for D7.

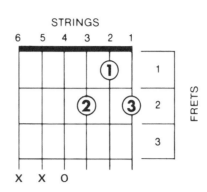

Strum once for each slash mark below.

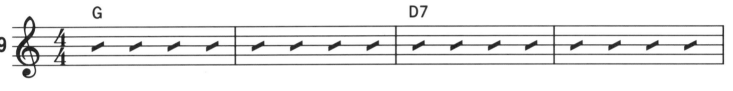

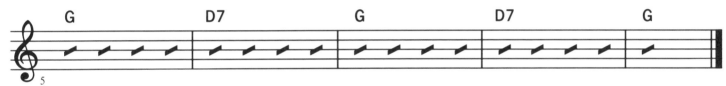

Review the fingering for the C chord and then practice Exercise 40 until you can play it well. Whenever you are moving between the C chord and the D7 chord, keep the first finger down.

12-BAR BLUES-ROCK ⑬ ⑭

Trade off strumming the chords and playing the melody with your teacher or a friend.

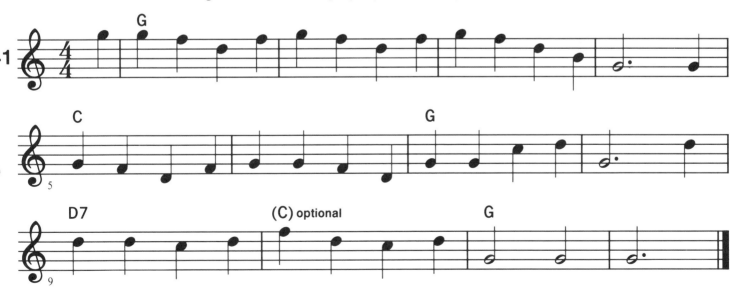

WORRIED MAN BLUES 15 16

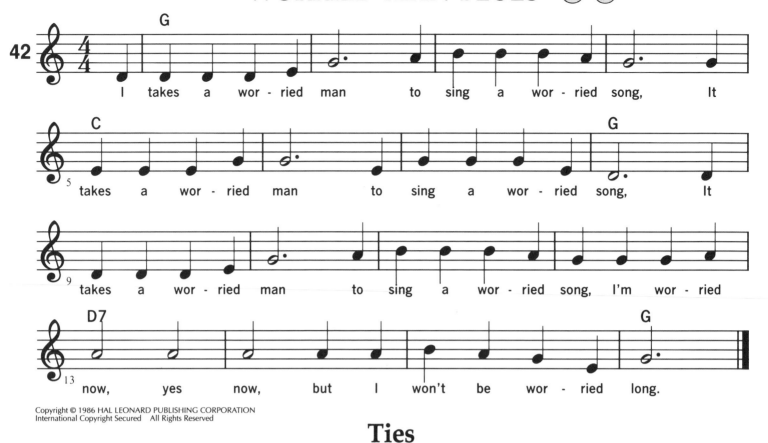

42

I takes a wor-ried man to sing a wor-ried song, It

takes a wor-ried man to sing a wor-ried song, It

takes a wor-ried man to sing a wor-ried song, I'm wor-ried

now, yes now, but I won't be wor-ried long.

Ties

A curved line which connects two notes of the same pitch is called a tie. The first note is struck and held for the value of both notes. The second note should not be played again. Look at the following illustration of tied notes.

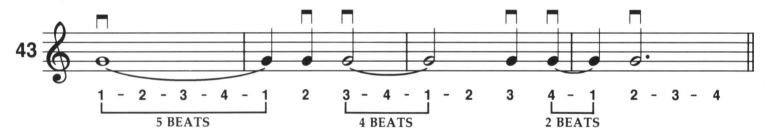

43

1 - 2 - 3 - 4 - 1   2   3 - 4 - 1 - 2   3   4 - 1   2 - 3 - 4

5 BEATS   4 BEATS   2 BEATS

AMAZING GRACE 17

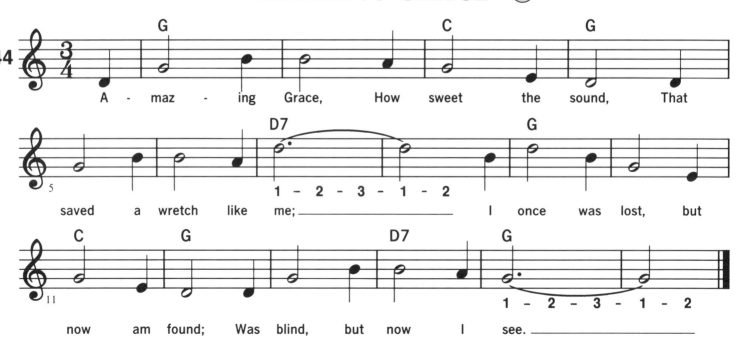

44

A - maz - ing Grace, How sweet the sound, That

saved a wretch like me; 1 - 2 - 3 - 1 - 2 *I once was lost, but*

now am found; Was blind, but now I see. 1 - 2 - 3 - 1 - 2

WHEN THE SAINTS GO MARCHING IN ⑱ ⑲

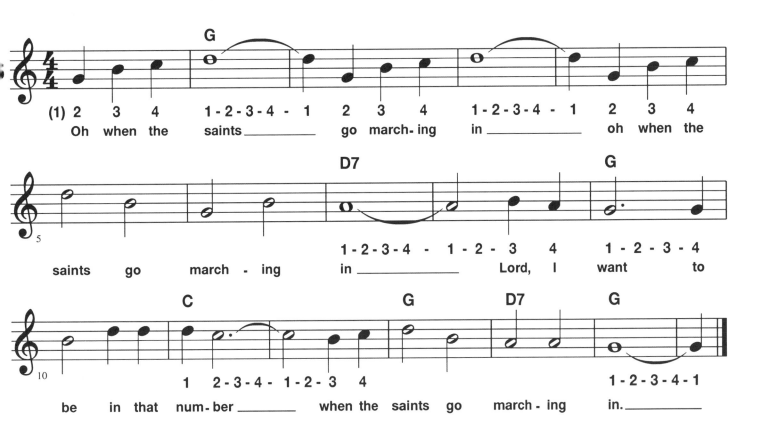

Remember that the chord letters shown in grey are to be played by your teacher.
You should play the melody only on this piece.

THE GYPSY GUITAR

NOTES ON THE FIFTH STRING

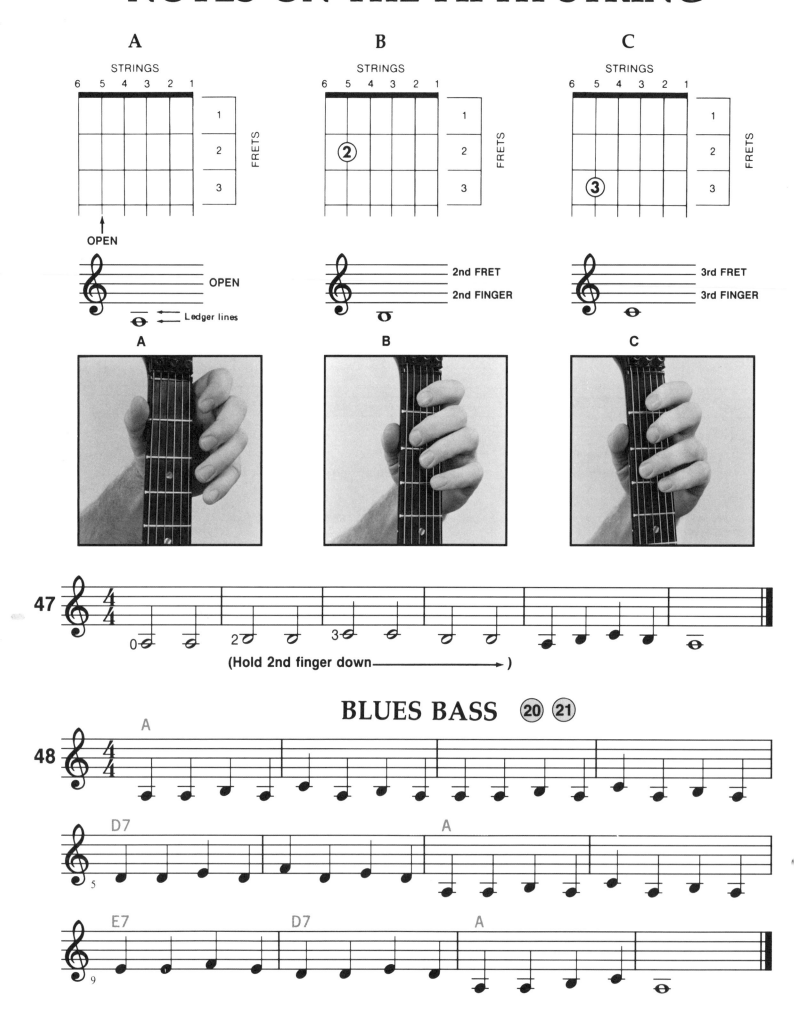

(Hold 2nd finger down ⟶)

BLUES BASS ⓴ ㉑

Practice these familiar melodies until you feel comfortable playing them. Remember to look ahead as you play so you can prepare for the next notes.

THE VOLGA BOATMAN

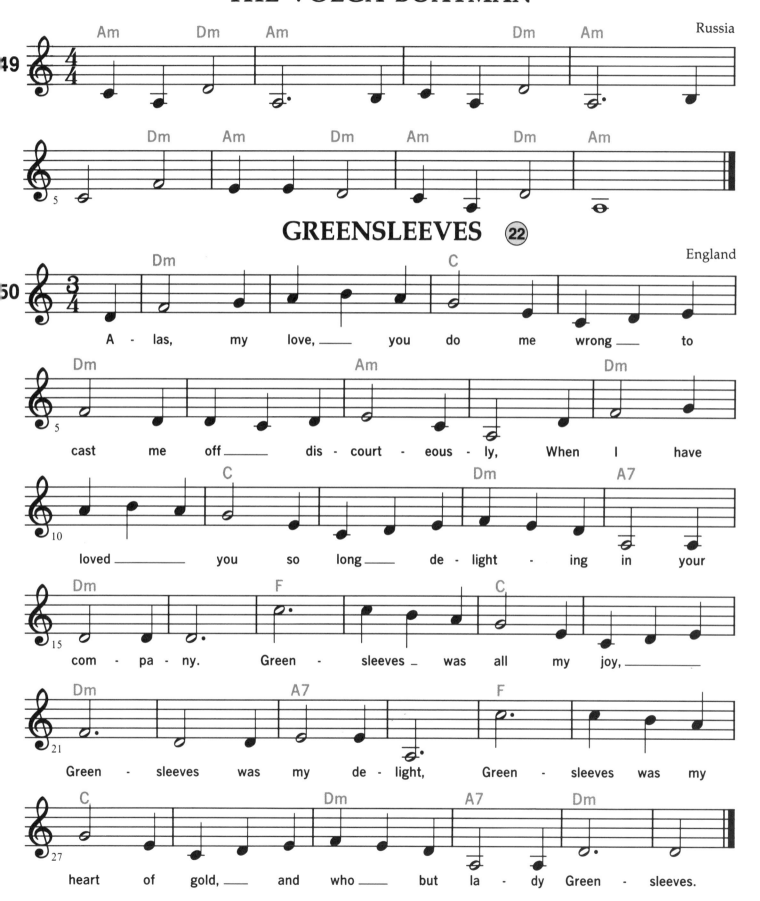

GREENSLEEVES

23

NOTES ON THE SIXTH STRING

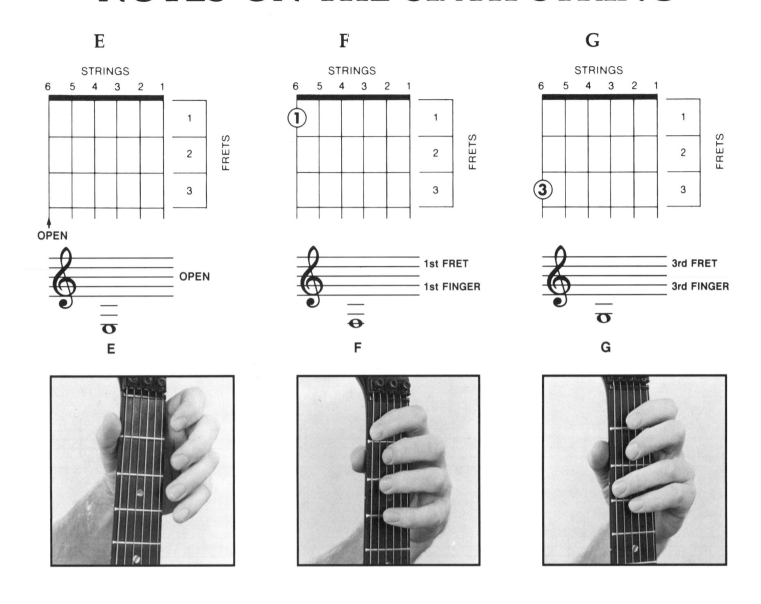

E F G

After you play these exercises, write the letter names below each note.

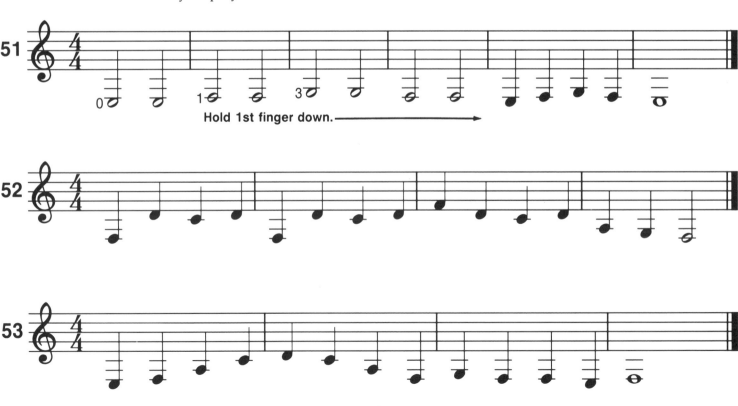

51 Hold 1st finger down. ➝

52

53

JOHNNY HAS GONE FOR A SOLDIER

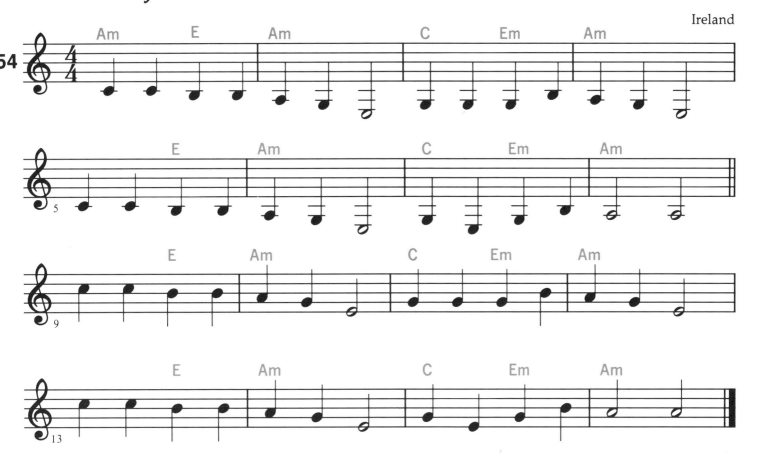

The interval between notes that have the same letter name and are eight notes apart is called an **octave**. The second half of **Johnny Has Gone for a Soldier** is written one octave higher than the first half.

Octaves

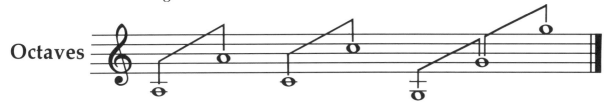

BASS ROCK

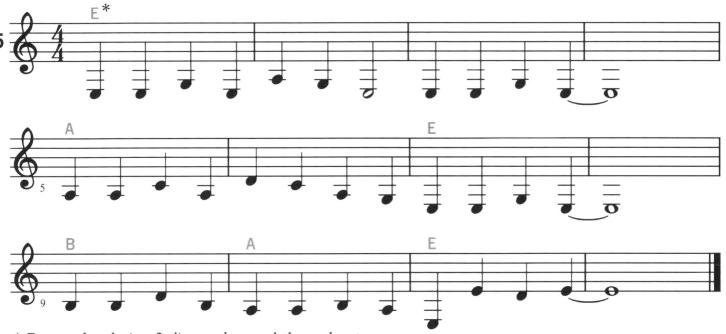

* Power chords (no 3rd) may be used throughout.

Half and Whole Steps

The distance between music tones is measured by half-steps and whole-steps. On your guitar the distance between one fret and the next fret is one half-step. The distance from one fret to the second fret in either direction is called a whole-step.

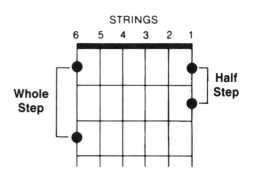

F-Sharp (F♯)

When a **sharp**(♯) is placed in front of a note, the note is raised one half-step and played one fret higher. A sharp placed before a note affects all notes on the same line or space that follow in that measure. Following are the three F♯s that appear on the fretboard to the right:

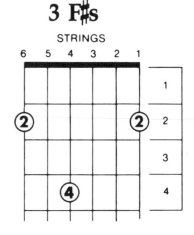

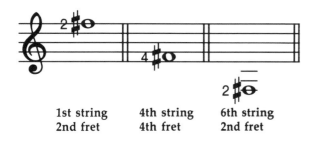

1st string	4th string	6th string
2nd fret	4th fret	2nd fret

Practice each of these finger exercises many times.

LONDONDERRY AIR ㉔

26

Key Signatures

Instead of writing a sharp sign before every F in a song, one sharp is placed at the beginning of the line. This is called a key signature and indicates that every F in the song should be played as F♯. In **Shenandoah** there will be an arrow above each F♯ to remind you to play F♯.

Shenandoah is written for 1, 2 or 3 guitar parts. Part 1 (the melody) will demand that you count out the tied notes accurately. Use a metronome or tap your foot and count aloud at first. With your teacher, other friends, or a tape recorder, play part 2 and the chords.

SHENANDOAH 25

Sea Shanty

Rests

Musical **rests** are moments of silence in music. Each type of note has a matching rest which has the same name and receives the same number of counts.

Whole	Half	Quarter
4 beats	2 beats	1 beat

A rest often requires that you stop the sound of your guitar strings with your right hand as is shown in the photo to the right. This process is called **dampening** the strings. Use the edge of your right hand to touch the strings, and work for a quiet economy of motion with little unnecessary movement.

As you play the following exercises that contain both notes and rests, count aloud using **numbers for the notes** and say the word, **"Rest," for each beat of silence.**

COUNT: 1 2 3 Rest 1 Rest 3 Rest Rest 2 3 4 1 - 2 Rest Rest

The letter **R** is used in place of the word, "Rest."

1 2 R R R 2 3 4 R R R R 1 R 3 4 1 - 2 - 3 R

1 R R 4 1 - 2 R R 1 2 3 - 4 1 R R R

In $\frac{3}{4}$ a complete measure of rest (3 counts) is written as a whole rest (➖).

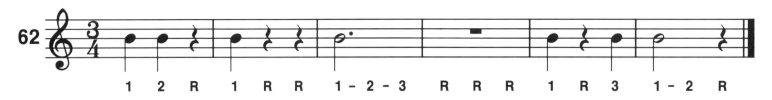

1 2 R 1 R R 1 - 2 - 3 R R R 1 R 3 1 - 2 R

ROCK 'N' REST 26

Count rests aloud:

JACK STUART 27

Scottish

29

THE FULL C, G and G7 CHORDS

When you began playing the C chord and the G7 chord, you used only three strings. You can play these chords on more strings and the sound will be much fuller. Study the illustrations below for the five-string C chord and the six-string G7 chord. Place each finger in the position shown and strum the chord several times.

C CHORD   ### G7 CHORD

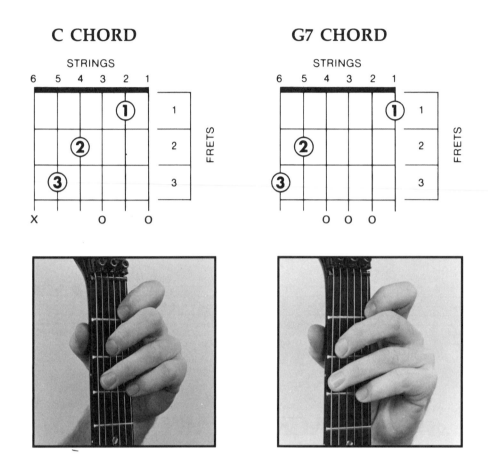

A double bar with two dots :‖ is a **repeat sign**, and it tells you to play the music a second time.

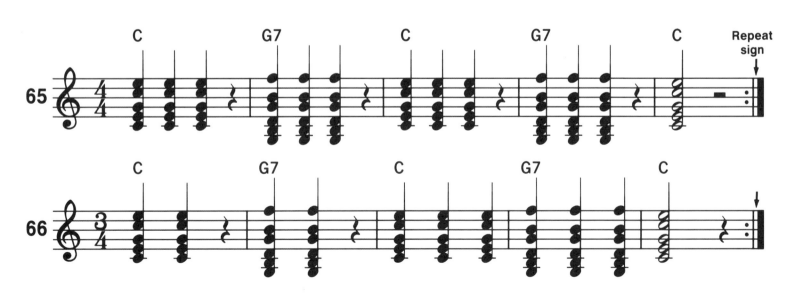

30

Earlier in the book you learned to play a three-string G chord. Now try the full six-string G chord for a fuller sound. Study the illustrations for the correct finger position. The formation using fingers 2, 3, and 4 will seem more difficult at first, but it will be easier to move to the C chord or the G7 chord. If your hand is small, use the formation with fingers 1, 2, and 3 or the G chord you learned earlier.

G CHORD   G CHORD

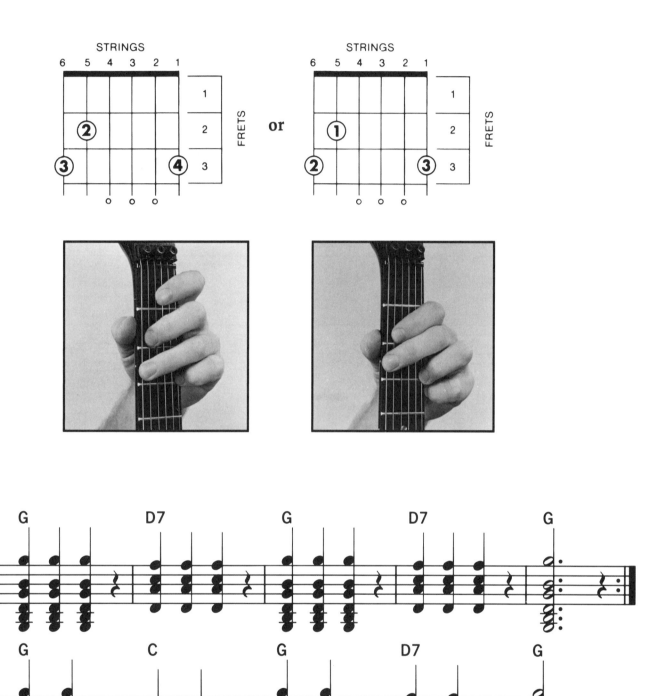

When you can play exercises 67 and 68 clearly and evenly, replace the rests with another strummed chord.

31

Practice trading off on melody and chords in these pieces.

WILL THE CIRCLE BE UNBROKEN

Country gospel

Will the cir - cle _____ be un - bro - ken, _____ by and
by, Lord, by and by? There's a
bet - ter _____ home a - wait - ing, _____ in the
sky, Lord, _____ in the _____ sky. _____

CORINNA 29

Blues

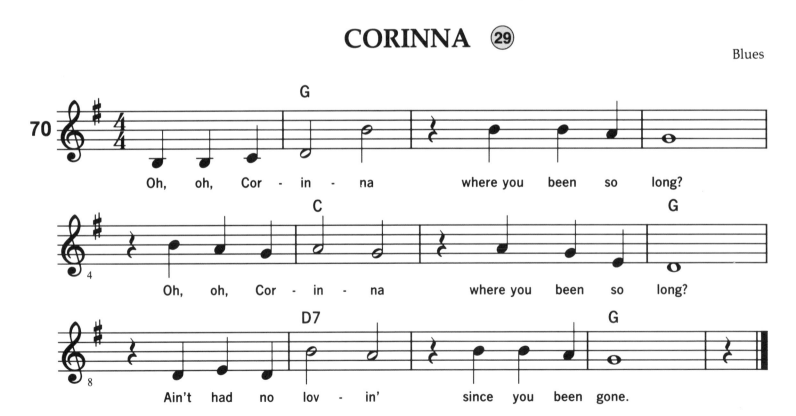

Oh, oh, Cor - in - na where you been so long?
Oh, oh, Cor - in - na where you been so long?
Ain't had no lov - in' since you been gone.

The Bass Note/Strum

When you played chords before, you strummed one chord for each beat in the measure. You can vary the strumming by alternating between a **bass note** (usually the **lowest note** of a chord and the **name** of the chord) and the **remainder of the chord**.

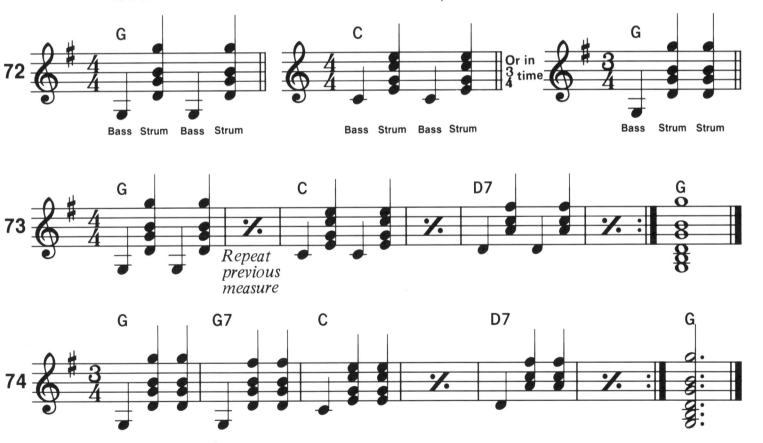

When you can play the bass-strum patterns with a steady rhythm, use them to accompany the previous songs or other songs you already know.

EIGHTH NOTES

An **eighth note** is half the length of a quarter note and gets ½ beat in $\frac{4}{4}$ or $\frac{3}{4}$.

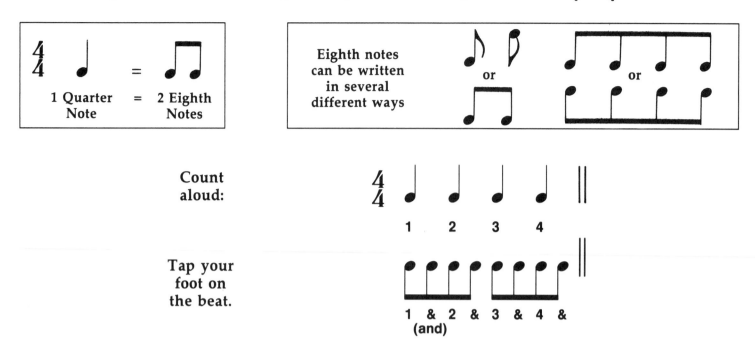

Count aloud:

Tap your foot on the beat.

Eighth notes are played with a **down (⊓) stroke** of the pick on the beat and an **up (∨) stroke** on the and (&).

75

Practice Exercise 76 with an alternating down and upstroke for all eighth notes and a down stroke for all quarter notes. It may help if you think that your pick is tied to your toe. When you tap your foot on the beat, the pick goes down. When your foot goes up on "and," your pick goes up.

76

Always practice slowly and steadily at first; then gradually increase the speed.

DRUNKEN SAILOR (31)

Sea Shanty

What will you do with a drunk-en sail-or? What will you do with a drunk-en sail-or?

What will you do with a drunk-en sail-or, ear-ly in the morn-ing?

FRERE JACQUES

France

Frè-re Jac-ques, frè-re Jac-ques, Dor-mez vous? dor-mez vous?
Are you sleep-ing? Are you sleep-ing? Broth-er John, Broth-er John,

Son-nez les ma-tin-es, son-nez les ma-tin-es, Din, din, don; din, din, don.
Morn-ing bells are ring-ing, Morn-ing bells are ring-ing, ding, dong, ding; ding, dong, ding.

* **Frere Jacques** can be played as a round. Enter when 1st player reaches the asterisk (*).
  Kookaburra can also be played as a 4-part round.

KOOKABURRA

Australia

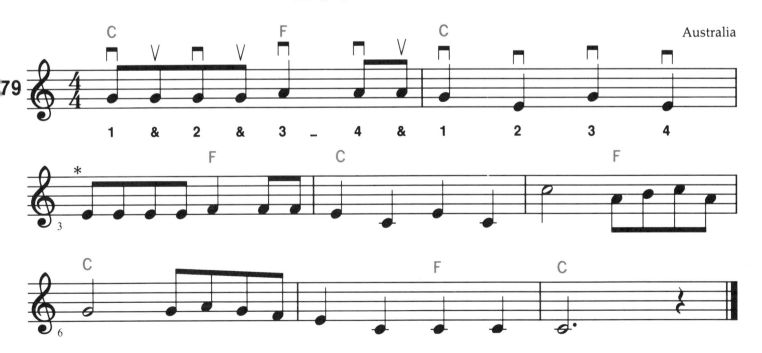

1 & 2 & 3 _ 4 & 1 2 3 4

Always check the key signature before you begin. All F's should be played F# in BOOGIE BASS.

BOOGIE BASS ③② ③③

3-PART ROUND

THE E MINOR CHORD

Em

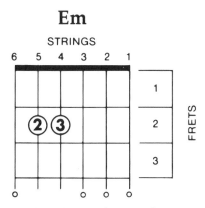

You've played the chords you learned in a variety of ways—as the full chord or only partial chords. The E minor chord can be played the same way. Study and play the example which shows the full six-string chord and a three-string partial chord.

When you are playing the E minor chord in the alternating bass note-chord pattern, use the sixth string for the bass note and the partial three-string chord. Practice the example until you can play it easily and clearly.

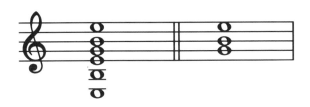

(6th string)

HEY, HO, NOBODY HOME

England

Hey, ho, no - bod - y home, Meat, nor drink, nor mon - ey have I none, Yet will I be mer - - - - ry

SHALOM CHAVERIM

Israel

Sha - lom, cha - ve - rim! Sha - lom, cha - ve - rim! Sha - lom, sha - lom! Le - hit - ra - ot, le - hit - ra - ot, Sha - lom, sha - lom.

*Play as a round if you wish.

37

Whenever two chords have a common finger position (one or more fingers stay in the same place), you should keep the common finger on the string. In the following progression there is a common finger between the G and Em chord and a common finger between the C and D7 chord. Practice the example until you can play it steadily and without any hesitation between chord changes.

Practice trading off on the melody and chords on **Molly Molone**. When you can play the chords easily, try a bass note with two after-strums that you learned in exercise number 74.

MOLLY MALONE 34

Ireland

MORE ADVANCED STRUMS

The down-up stroke pattern you have already played on eighth notes can also be applied to strums. As you practice strumming the following exercises, keep your wrist relaxed and flexible. The down-up motion will be much faster and easier if you use down-up motion of the wrist only rather than of the entire arm. This wrist motion feels a little like shaking water off the hand.

BASIC DOWN-UP STRUM

STRUM VARIATIONS

A variation of the basic down-up strum misses the upstroke or "and" of the first beat. Remember to keep the down-up motion going and miss the strings on the "and" of beat one.

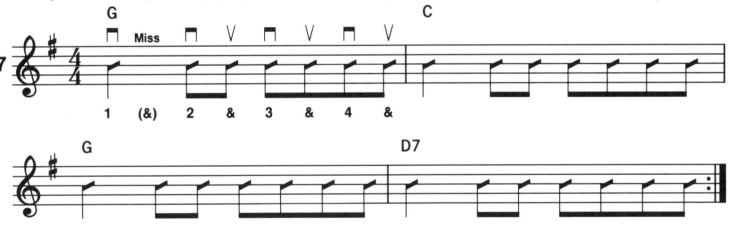

This variation misses two up strokes. Continue to strum but miss the strings on the "and" of beats one and three.

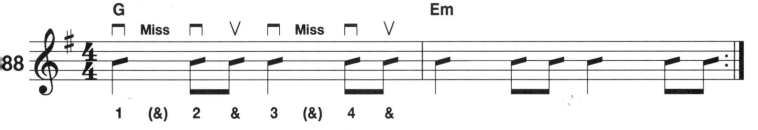

On "Simple Gifts" you can play the melody (Part 1), the harmony line (Part 2), or the chordal accompaniment.

Practice these strums before playing "Simple Gifts."

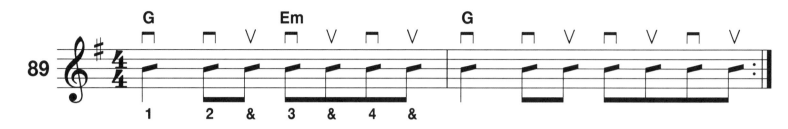

SIMPLE GIFTS 〔35〕〔36〕

Shaker song

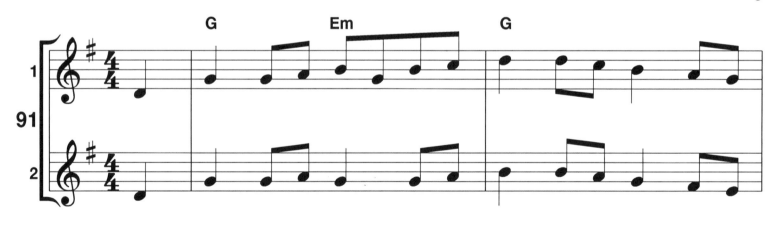

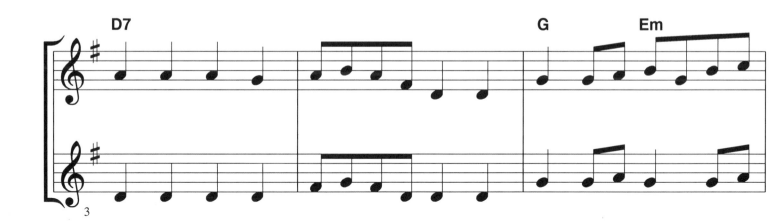

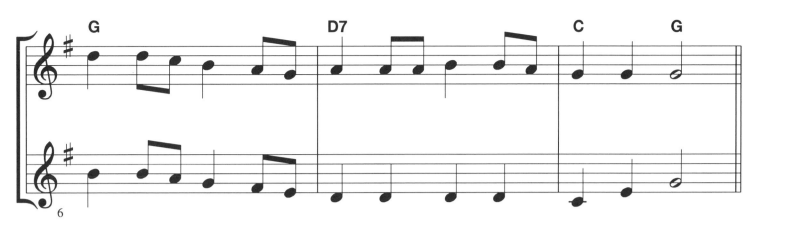

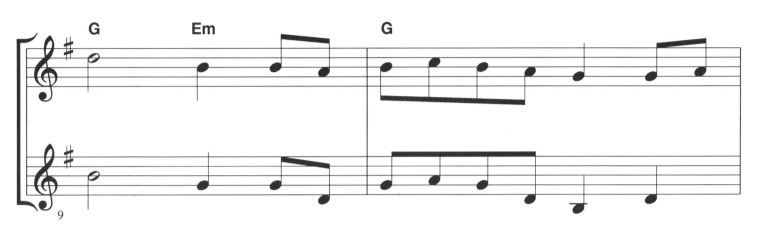

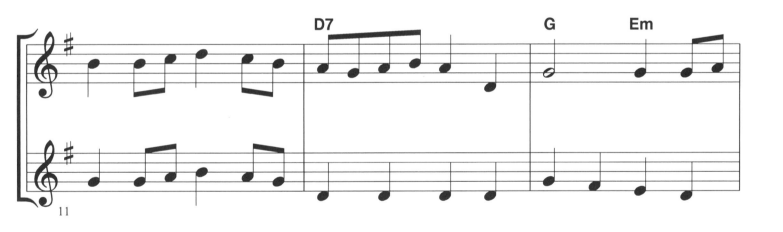

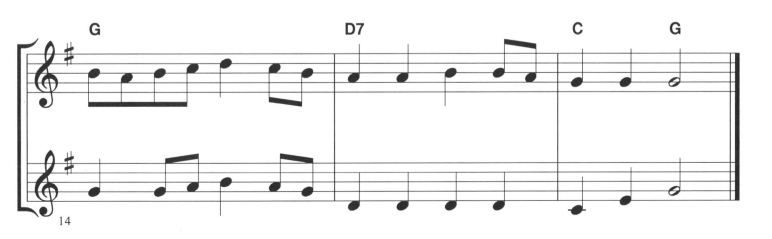

BASS-MELODY SOLOS

This style solo was developed on the Carter family recordings. The melody is played in the bass and long notes (𝅗𝅥 𝅗𝅥. or 𝅝) are filled in with strums. Emphasize the bass melody notes and play lightly on the strums.

ROW, ROW, ROW YOUR BOAT

*You can hold your 1st finger down throughout the entire solo if you wish.

WORRIED MAN BLUES ㊲ ㊳

Takes a wor-ried man ____ to sing a wor-ried song, ____

Takes a wor-ried man ____ to sing a wor-ried song, ____

Takes a wor-ried man ____ to sing a wor-ried song, I'm wor-ried

now, ____ but I won't be wor-ried long. ____

WHEN THE SAINTS GO MARCHING IN

Oh when the saints_____ go march-ing in _____ oh when the

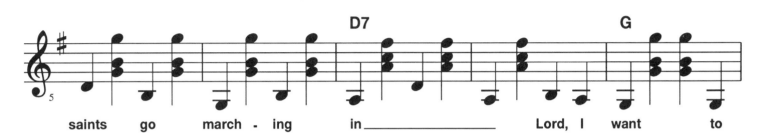

saints go march - ing in _____ Lord, I want to

be in that num-ber when the saints go march - ing in.

When you feel that these solos are coming along well, you might wish to try a variation on the strums. Instead of a single down stroke ( ), play a down-up stroke ( ). Practice this exercise; then put the down-up stroke in the solos.

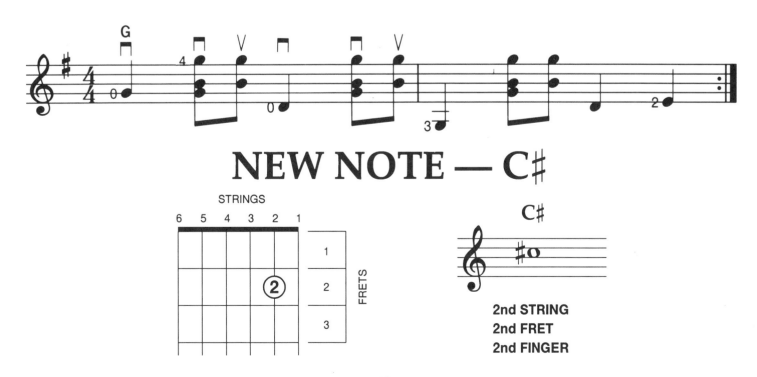

NEW NOTE — C♯

STRINGS

C♯

2nd STRING
2nd FRET
2nd FINGER

MINUET IN G ㊴ ㊵

J.S. BACH
(Guitar 2 arr.
by W. Schmid)

95

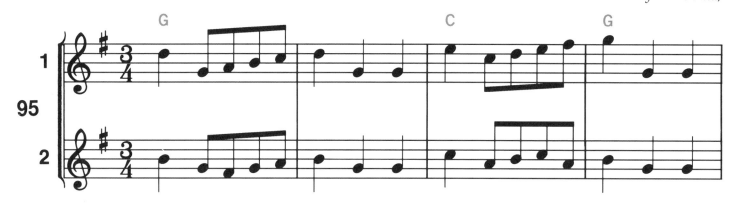

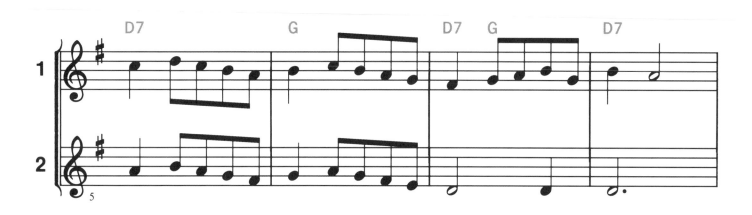

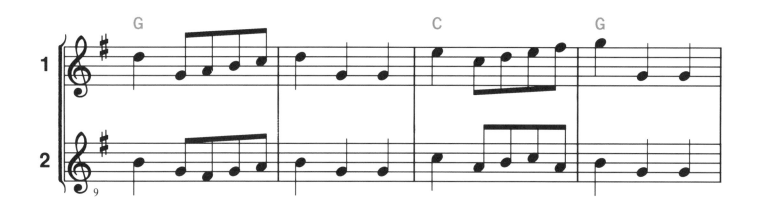

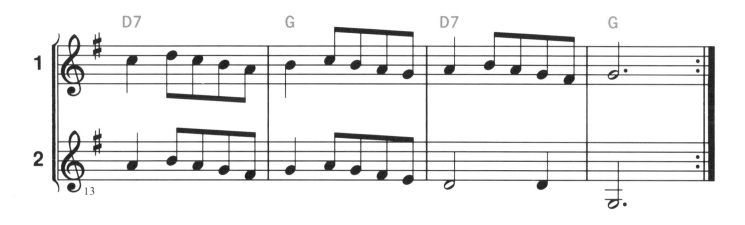

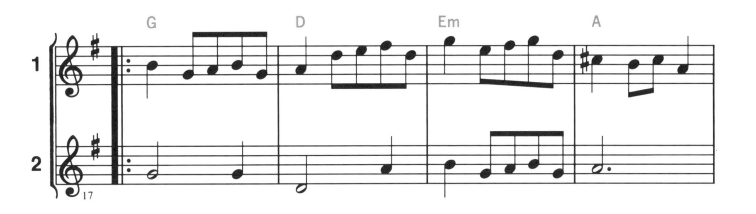

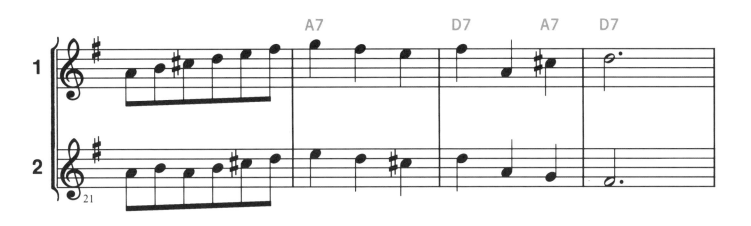

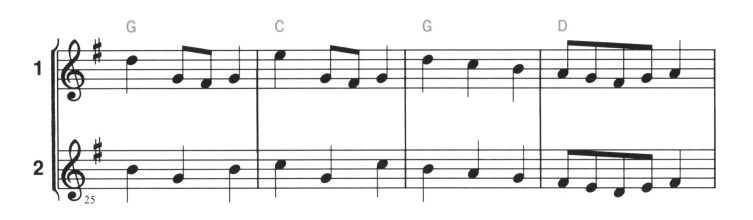

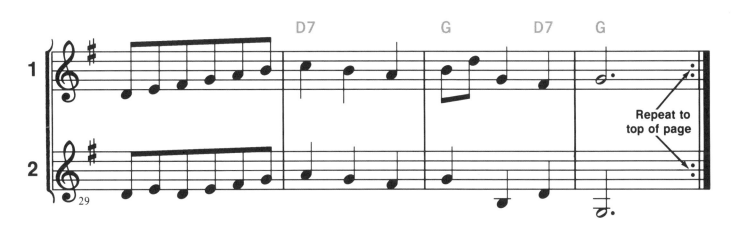

Repeat to top of page

45

GUITAR ENSEMBLE 41

3-part round

After learning this Russian "Tumba" round, you may wish to play it with two or three other guitarists. Each player begins when the previous player has reached line 3 at the asterisk. A more advanced player such as your teacher may play the chords (repeating them throughout). Play the round three times through with gradually accelerating speed.

CHORD CHART

In this chart you will find the chords learned in this book as well as several other common chords you may see in music you are playing.

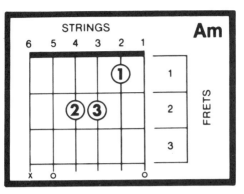

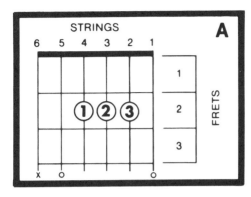

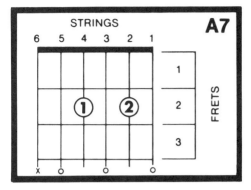

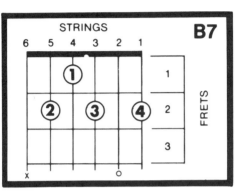

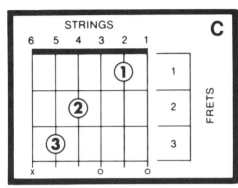

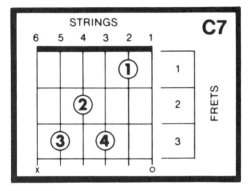

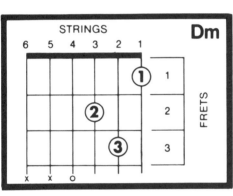

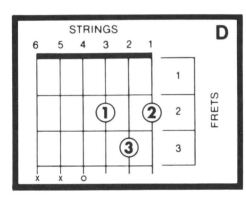

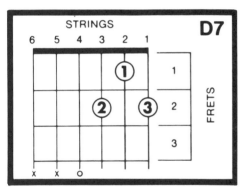

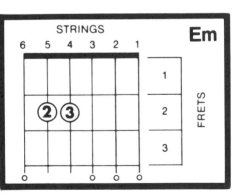

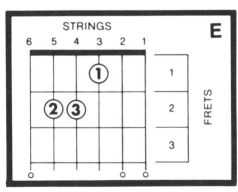

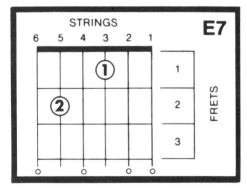

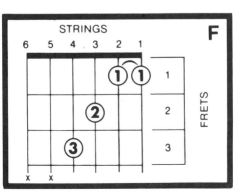

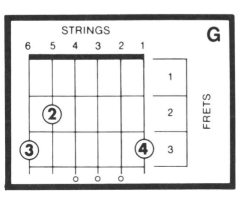

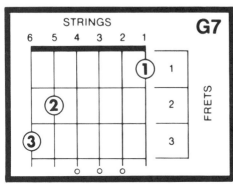

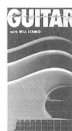

Hal Leonard GUITAR METHOD ™

by Will Schmid

Will Schmid has gained the reputation as an outstanding guitar teacher and performer throughout the United States. He received his BA from Luther College and his PhD from the Eastman School of Music. While teaching at the University of Kansas, he created and performed a series of programs entitled "Folk Music Americana" for National Public Radio. He is currently Associate Professor of Music Education at the University of Wisconsin-Milwaukee and serves on the editorial staff of Hal Leonard Publishing Corporation.

Contents

Keys and Major Scales. 2
  Yankee Doodle in C. 4
  Yankee Doodle in G. 4
Intervals 4
Chords 5
  Yankee Doodle in D. 6
The D and A7 Chords 7
  I Know Where I'm Going. 8
  Polly Wolly Doodle 8
  Michael, Row The Boat Ashore 9
  Kumbayah. 10
  My Bonnie Lies Over The Ocean 11
Syncopation. 12
  Calypso Bay 12
  Rock-A-My Soul 12
  He's Got The Whole World In His Hands 13
  Oh, Mary Don't You Weep. 14
  Little David Play On Your Harp 14
More Advanced Strums 15
  Rock Island Line 16
The Am7 Chord. 17
  Simple Gifts 17
The A Chord. 18
  Follow The Drinkin' Gourd 18
Syncopated Strums 19
  Pay Me My Money Down 20
The F Chord. 21
  Who's Gonna Shoe Your Pretty Little Feet. . . 21
  The Streets Of Laredo. 22
  Mama Don't 'Low. 23
The Am Chord. 24
  Nine Hundred Miles. 24

The Dm Chord. 25
  Sinner Man. 25
  Stewball 26-28
The Minor Scale 29
  Frère Jacques 29
  Wayfaring Stranger 30
  Black Is The Color Of My True Love's Hair. . . 31
  Bound For The Promised Land 31
The E Chord. 32
  Joshua Fought The Battle Of Jericho. 32
  Hava Nagila 33
The B7 Chord. 34
  The Blues 34
New Note . . . A♯-B♭ 35
  24-Hour Blues 35
New Note . . . C♯ 36
  All The Pretty Little Horses 37
Arpeggios. 37
  Keep Your Hand On The Plow 38
  Banks Of The Ohio 40
  Roll In My Sweet Baby's Arms. 41
  The Golden Vanity. 42
  The Minstrel Boy. 43
  The Ash Grove. 43
  Irish Washerwoman. 44
  Patsy-Ory-Ory-Aye. 44
  Wee Cooper O'Fife 45
  Jesu, Joy Of Man's Desiring. 45
Modified Chords 46
  Plaisir D'Amour 46
Chord Chart 47

HAL•LEONARD
CORPORATION
7777 W. BLUEMOUND RD. P.O. BOX 13819 MILWAUKEE, WI 53213

Keys and Scales

Each piece of music is based upon a particular series of notes. The arrangement in steps of these notes is called a scale. Depending upon the arrangement of whole-steps and half-steps each scale has a particular name.

The first type of scale you'll be learning is a major scale. It has eight notes with the following whole and half-step pattern.

The C Major Scale

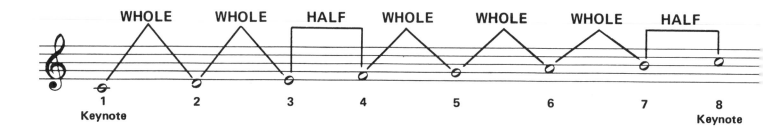

Notice that there is a half-step between notes 3 and 4 and again between 7 and 8.

A scale is named by the first and last note so the scale above is a C Scale. The particular "step pattern" shown above is for a major scale—so that the full name of the scale is the C Major Scale.

You learned in Book I that a sharp raises a note one half-step. There is also a sign called a flat (♭) which lowers a note one half-step. If a scale has no sharps or flats and begins on C, it is in the key of C. Likewise if you look at a song and there are no sharps or flats in the key signature, the song is probably in the key of C.

Practice this ascending and descending C Major scale and listen carefully.

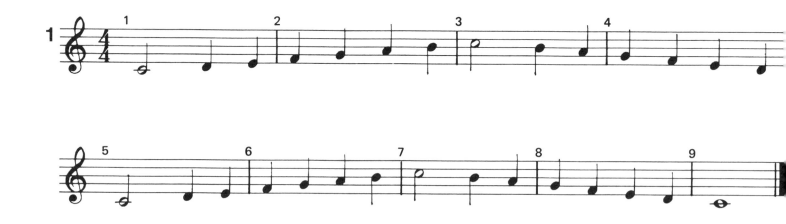

The G Major Scale

If you build a scale on the keynote, G, the whole and half-step pattern still looks like this.

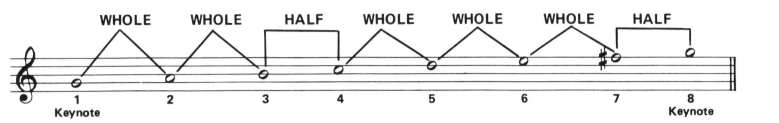

In this scale, however, you must add a sharp to F to create a half-step between notes 7 and 8. This is a G Major scale because it begins and ends on G. The key signature for G Major is one sharp (F♯).

Now play the G Major scale up and down two octaves.

Transposing

To develop your skills as a musician you will want to be able to play in more than one key. When you begin a song or scale on a different note, you are transposing, moving the whole and half-step pattern to a different note.

Here is "Yankee Doodle" written in the key of C and then transposed to the key of G. Remember to check the key signature before you begin any song so you will play the correct notes.

YANKEE DOODLE IN C

YANKEE DOODLE IN G

Intervals

When we discussed scales on page 2, we gave each scale note a number. You can use these numbers to determine the interval or distance between notes.

The interval between steps one and two is a second, from one to three a third, from one to four a fourth, etc.

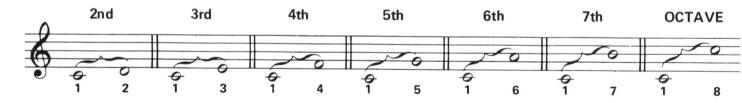

You can also start with a note other than the key note and determine intervals. Call that note one, then count up or down (alternating line/space, space/line) to find the interval.

4

Chords

Chords are stacked intervals. A three-note chord is called a triad and consists of two stacked thirds. They are named for their bottom note or root.

A single letter above a chord G, D, C, etc., indicates that chord is a major chord. When the letter is followed by a small "m," the chord is a minor chord. This means that the third of the chord is one half-step lower than the major chord.

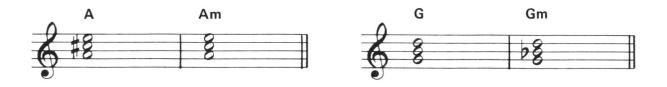

When a seventh is added above the root of the chord, it is called a seventh chord, indicated by G7, D7, etc.

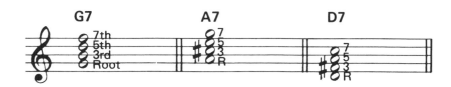

Because the guitar has six strings, many chords have notes doubled or tripled.

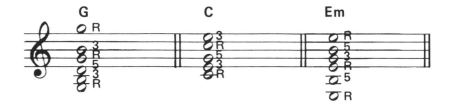

The D Major Scale

Now let's learn a new major scale and key signature, D.

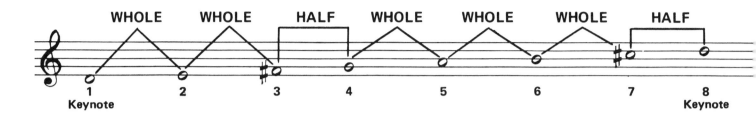

Since there is an F♯ and a C♯ in the D Major scale, the key signature for D Major is two sharps (F♯ and C♯).

Practice the D Major scale ascending and descending. After you can play it slowly, increase the speed and play alternating down-up strokes. This key is used frequently in guitar music so learn the fingering pattern well. For extra practice transposing, play "Yankee Doodle" in the key of D.

YANKEE DOODLE IN D

Supplement this book with a Hal Leonard's
MORE EASY POP MELODIES

As you progress through Book 2, you will have the opportunity to play additional songs from Hal Leonard's MORE EASY POP MELODIES. Each supplementary song is carefully coordinated with the instructional material in this method. The title and page reference for these songs appears at the bottom of selected pages in this book.

The D Chord and the A7 Chord

Two of the chords most commonly used in the key of D Major are the D chord and the A7 chord. Learn the fingering for each of these chords; then practice the exercises below.

D CHORD

A7 CHORD

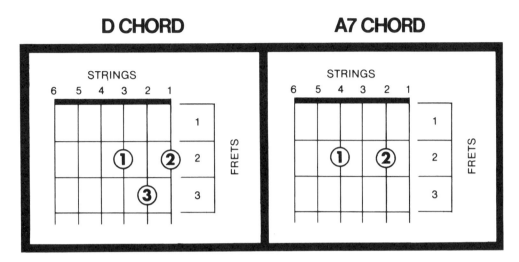

The D chord is a four-string chord. When you play this chord, it is very important that you keep your left-hand fingers arched and press with the very tips of your fingers.

To play the A7 chord, place your left-hand fingers in position as shown in the illustration and strum the first five strings. Be sure that the guitar neck does not touch your left palm.

When you are playing the alternating bass strum (bass note followed by the chord), use the open 4th string as the bass note of the D chord. The bass note of the A7 chord is the open 5th string.

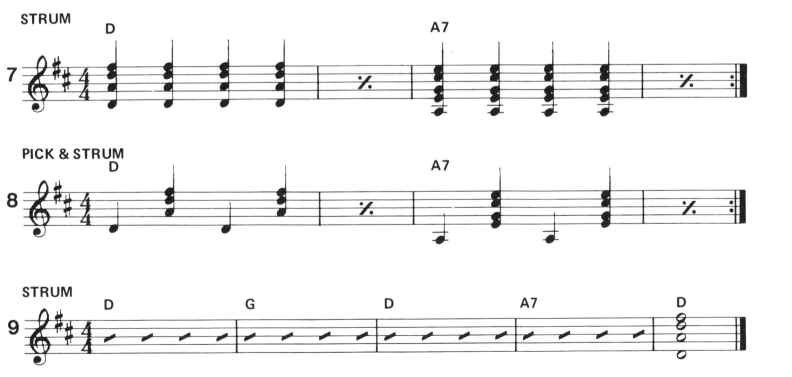

Practice the melodies of each of the following songs; then sing the melody as you strum the chords.

I KNOW WHERE I'M GOING

Be sure to play downstrokes (⊓) and upstrokes (∨) on the eighth notes in "Polly Wolly Doodle." Remember that high A is played with the fourth finger.

POLLY WOLLY DOODLE

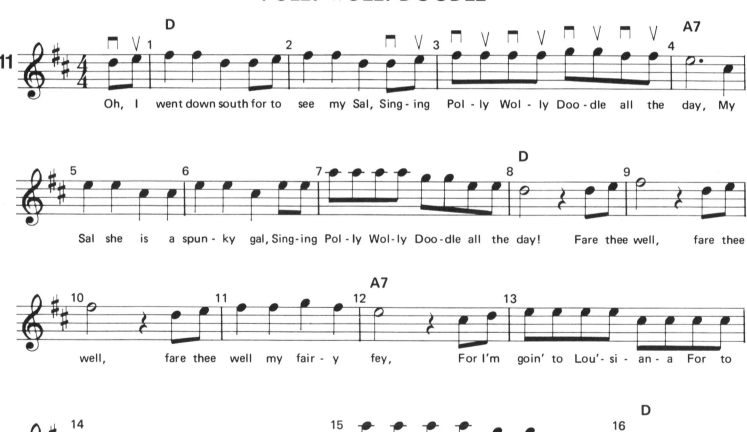

You are now ready to play THE RAINBOW CONNECTION, pg. 2 of Hal Leonard's MORE EASY POP MELODIES.

Dotted Quarter Notes

You've already learned that a dot after a note increases the value by one-half.

$$\text{♩} \quad + \quad \cdot \quad = \quad \text{♩·}$$

2 BEATS + 1 BEAT = 3 BEATS

A dot after a quarter note also increases its value by one-half.

$$\text{♩} \quad + \quad \cdot \quad = \quad \text{♩·}$$

1 BEAT + ½ BEAT = 1½ BEATS

Practice the exercises below and count aloud as you play. Whisper the counts that are in parentheses and let the held (tied or dotted) note ring while you whisper. Measures 2 and 3 in the next two exercises should sound exactly alike.

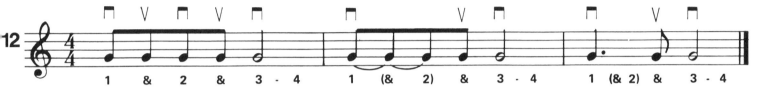

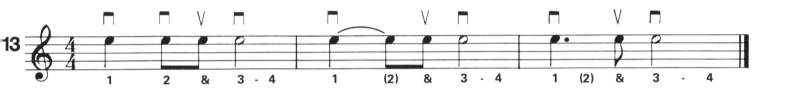

First practice playing the melody to "Michael, Row The Boat Ashore"; then sing as you strum the chords.

MICHAEL, ROW THE BOAT ASHORE

KUMBAYAH

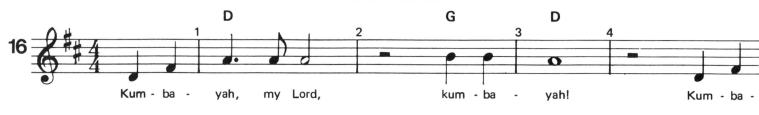

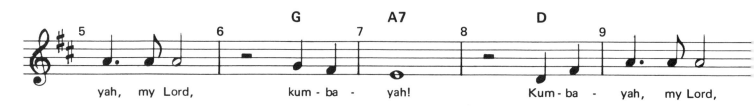

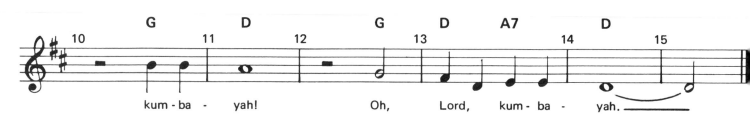

When you are strumming chords in this song or any others, be sure to play steadily and without any hesitation between chords. If you are having difficulty changing chords smoothly, practice them slowly at first.

MY BONNIE LIES OVER THE OCEAN

Syncopation

One form of syncopation is the stressing or accenting of notes on the "ands" of beats. Sometimes the accent is a result of tying eighth notes together or of placing quarter notes on the off-beats. Practice each exercise slowly and carefully. Increase the speed after you are sure you can play the rhythm correctly.

Keep the down-up stroke going throughout the exercise. When you see a count in parentheses, simply miss the string and let the sound ring. By doing this you will play the syncopated pattern with the correct stroke of the pick.

For extra practice, play all of the syncopation exercises on all of the open strings.

Now play Exercise 24 which uses syncopation in the melody. After you can play it well, strum the chords as you sing the melody.

CALYPSO BAY

First play the melody; then sing as you strum the chords for the next song.

ROCK-A-MY SOUL

Rock-a-my soul in the bos-om of A - bra-ham, Rock-a-my soul in the bos-om of A - bra-ham,

Rock-a - my soul in the bos-om of A - bra-ham, Oh, rock - a-my soul.

You are now ready to play ALL SHOOK UP, pg. 3 of Hal Leonard's MORE EASY POP MELODIES.

Practice the new syncopation patterns in the next two exercises many times. These patterns are used in "He's Got The Whole World In His Hands."

Be sure to play both melody and chord strums on this song.

HE'S GOT THE WHOLE WORLD IN HIS HANDS

He's got the whole world__ in His hands,__ He's got the whole wide world __ in His hands, He's got the

whole world __ in His hands,__ He's got the whole world in His hands. _____

The verse of a song was originally the part of a song sung by a soloist and the chorus was the part sung by a chorus or group of singers. The chorus was also repetitious music to fit with the repeated text. It has developed so that the chorus is usually the most recognized and remembered portion of a song and the verse usually tells a story.

OH, MARY DON'T YOU WEEP

If I could_ I sure-ly would,_ Stand on the rock where the Mo-ses stood._ Pha-raoh's ar - my got

drown - ded, Oh, Ma - ry don't you weep. Oh, Ma - ry don't you weep, don't you mourn,

Oh, Ma - ry don't you weep, don't you mourn, Pha-roah's ar-my got drown - ded, Oh, Ma-ry don't you weep.

You are already familiar with the dotted double bar (:||) that indicates the repeat of the section before it. When you see two repeat bars (||:   :||), you should repeat the music between them.

You will also see first and second endings ([1 |2   ]) in this song. Play the first ending the first time through the song. Go back to the repeat sign and play the section again. On the second time through, skip the first ending and go on to the second ending.

LITTLE DAVID PLAY ON YOUR HARP

You are now ready to play LONGER, pg. 4 of Hal Leonard's MORE EASY POP MELODIES.

More Advanced Strums

The down-up stroke pattern you have already played on eighth notes can also be applied to strums. As you practice strumming the following exercises, keep your wrist relaxed and flexible. The down-up motion will be much faster and easier if you use down-up motion of the wrist only rather than of the entire arm. This wrist motion feels a little like shaking water off the hand.

To keep the beat as you're playing strums, continue the down-upstroke. When you have a note longer than one eighth note, simply miss the string on that strum. The next note or strum will then have the correct downstroke or upstroke.

BASIC DOWN-UP STRUM

VARIATION I

Variation I of the basic down-up strum misses the upstroke or "and" of the first beat. Remember to keep the down-up motion going and miss the strings on the "and" of beat one.

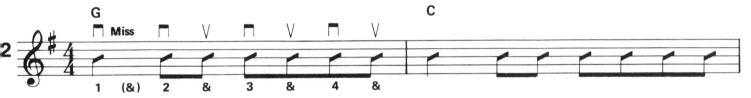

VARIATION II

Variation II misses two upstrokes. Continue to strum but miss the strings on the "and" of beats one and three.

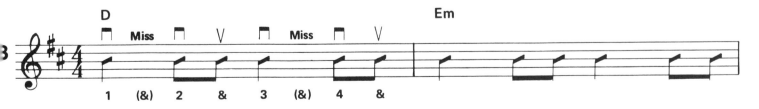

Try all of the strums on the following songs until you find the pattern you like best.
The strum rhythm is not always the same as the melodic rhythm.

Be sure to practice the melody first; then strum the chords as you sing. Remember:
D.C. al Fine means to go back to the beginning and play to Fine, the end.

ROCK ISLAND LINE

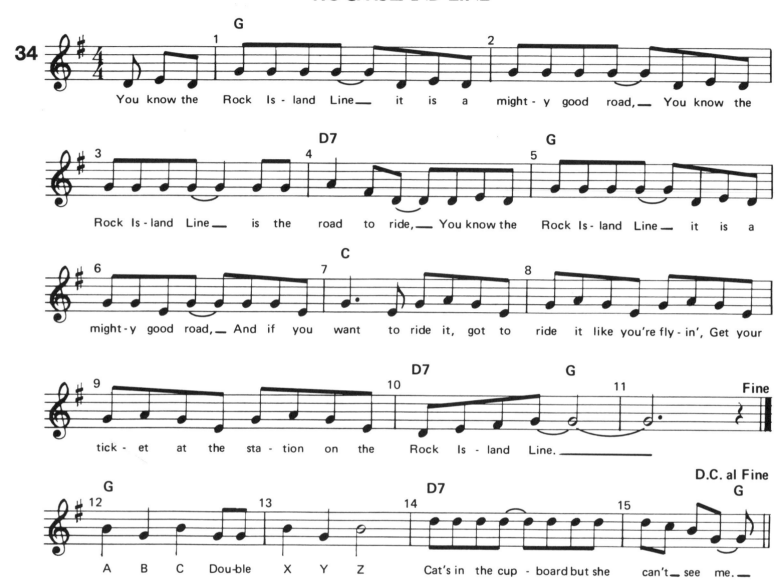

34

You know the Rock Is-land Line__ it is a might-y good road,__ You know the

Rock Is-land Line__ is the road to ride,__ You know the Rock Is-land Line__ it is a

might-y good road,__ And if you want to ride it, got to ride it like you're fly-in', Get your

tick-et at the sta-tion on the Rock Is-land Line._____

A B C Dou-ble X Y Z Cat's in the cup-board but she can't__ see me.__

The Am7 Chord

The Am7 chord is an easy chord to play. Check the fingering illustration and try the chord. The bass note for the alternating bass note/chord pattern is the open fifth string.

Am7

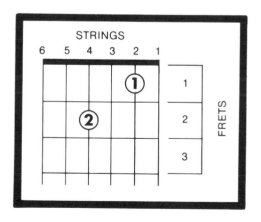

You are now ready to play EDELWEISS, pg. 5 of Hal Leonard's MORE EASY POP MELODIES.

When the chords change every two beats, you should use a strum pattern that takes two beats to complete such as Variation II.

As you develop your skills, you should vary your strumming to fit a song. For example in measures 7 and 8 and 15 and 16 you play the strumming pattern shown so the section will sound more complete.

In the song "Simple Gifts" the chords change more frequently than in many of the songs you've played so far. You should practice moving from one chord to the next until you can make the changes without hesitation.

Practice the melody until you can play it well.

SIMPLE GIFTS

You are now ready to play HEY JUDE, pg. 6 of Hal Leonard's MORE EASY POP MELODIES.

The A Chord

Study the illustration for the A chord. The bass string for this chord is the fifth string.

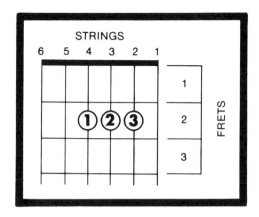

In this song, you have to change from the Em chord to the A chord quickly. Practice the following exercise until you can play it without hesitation. Begin slowly and gradually increase the speed.

Use the strumming pattern shown in Exercise 38 in the first four measures of Exercise 39. From measure 5 to measure 16 the strumming pattern of the last measure of Exercise 38 will sound good.

FOLLOW THE DRINKIN' GOURD

You are now ready to play GET BACK, pg. 8 of Hal Leonard's MORE EASY POP MELODIES.

Syncopated Strums

You have played the rhythms of the new strum variations in melodic form. Remember to keep the down-up motion going always and simply miss the string on notes longer than one eighth note.

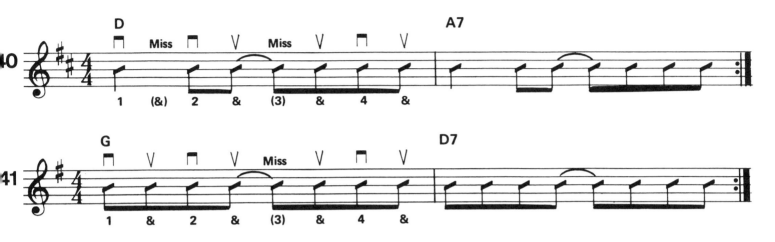

Now try this pattern using different chords.

After playing the melody to "Marianne," use the strumming pattern above as you sing the melody.

MARIANNE

All day, all night, Mar - ri - anne,_____ Down by __ the sea - side __ sift - ing sand;_____ E - ven lit - tle child - ren __ love Mar - ri - anne,_____ Down by __ the sea - side __ sift - ing sand._____

Playing the syncopated strums alone is easy. When you are strumming as you are singing the melody, it becomes a little more difficult. Practice the next exercises several different ways:

1. Play the syncopation exercise.

2. Play the melody of Exercise 45 several times until you can sing it easily.

3. Sing the melody as you strum quarter notes.

4. Sing the melody as you strum the syncopated strum.

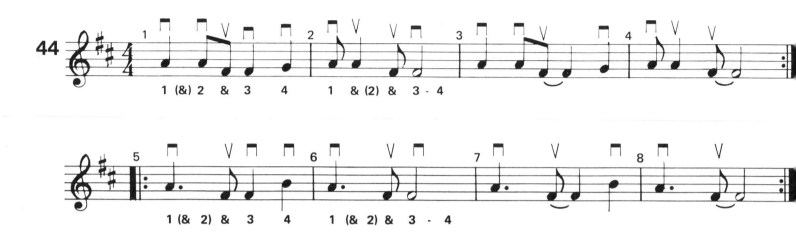

PAY ME MY MONEY DOWN

I thought I heard the big boss say "Pay me my mon-ey down!

Pay me or go to jail, Pay me my mon-ey down!" "Pay me, oh pay me,

Pay me my mon-ey down! Pay me or go to jail, Pay me my mon-ey down!"

The F Chord

To play the F chord your first finger will press two strings instead of one string as usual. The underside of the finger will contact the string at the first fret. Fingers two and three are arched and press the correct strings with the tips only. Strum the first four strings, and play a fourth string bass note.

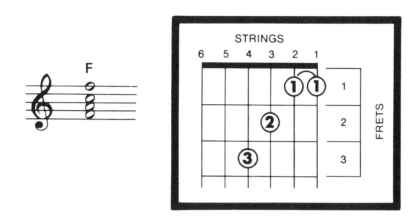

Practice the following exercise before going on. Keep the rhythm steady and don't hesitate when you change chords.

WHO'S GONNA SHOE YOUR PRETTY LITTLE FEET?

You are now ready to play TICKET TO RIDE, pg. 9 of Hal Leonard's MORE EASY POP MELODIES.

Practice the melody and chord changes until you can play them well.

THE STREETS OF LAREDO

As I _____ walked out in the streets of La - re - do, As
I walked out in La - re - do one day, I
spied a young cow - boy all wrapped in white lin - en, All
wrapped in white lin - en as cold as the clay.

For songs written in ¾ time, you can use the following strumming pattern. It is a variation of the alternating bass note/chord pattern with the bass note on the first beat only.

After you can play this exercise without any hesitation between the chords, use the strumming pattern for "The Streets of Laredo."

MAMA DONT 'LOW

2. Mama don't 'low no banjo playing 'round here, (twice)

I don't care what mama don't 'low, gonna play my banjo anyhow,

Mama don't 'low no banjo playing 'round here.

3. 4. & 5. Use other instruments such as kazoo, washboard, gutbucket, etc.

You are now ready to play WITH A LITTLE HELP, pg. 10 of Hal Leonard's MORE EASY POP MELODIES.

The Am Chord

The A minor chord will be very similar to the Am7 chord which you have already learned. Add the third finger on the third string. The bass string for the Am chord is the open fifth string.

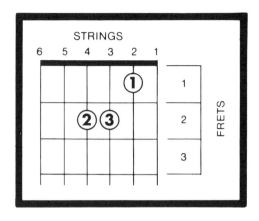

First play the melody; then accompany your singing by strumming any of the patterns on page 15 or 19.

NINE HUNDRED MILES

Well, I'm rid-ing on that train, I've got tears in my eyes, _____ Trying to read a let-ter from my home. _____ If that train is run-ning right I'll be home to-mor-row night, 'Cause I'm nine hun-dred miles from my home, _____ And I hate to hear that lone-some whis-tle blow. _____

You are now ready to play AND I LOVE HER, pg. 11 of Hal Leonard's MORE EASY POP MELODIES.

The Dm Chord

Place your fingers carefully on the positions indicated for the D minor chord. Strum only strings one through four. The bass note for the Dm chord is the open fourth string.

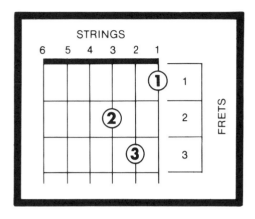

Practice changing chords in the following. Play slowly and steadily so there is no hesitation between chords.

SINNER MAN

Oh, sin-ner man, where you gon-na run to? Oh, sin-ner man, where you gon-na run to?

Oh, sin-ner man, where you gon-na run to? All on that day?

When you know both the melody and chords well, practice the bass note/strum pattern below. Play this pattern as you sing the melody.

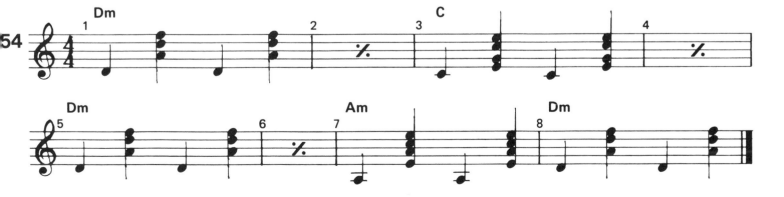

You are now ready to play LONG AND WINDING ROAD, pg. 12 of Hal Leonard's MORE EASY POP MELODIES.

There are many ways you can play a song to add variety. The easiest way is to play the melody only. You can also play an alternating bass note/strum pattern; a strum variation; alternating bass note pattern; or a combination of the melody and chords. On the next three pages several versions of "Stewball" are introduced. Be sure to practice all of them until you can play them smoothly and easily. After you study how each version is constructed, try to develop different arrangements of other songs you know.

When there are several verses to a song, the additional verses are often typed in a group below the song. In this book the syllable that falls on the first beat of each measure is underlined to help you keep your place in the song.

Be sure you know the melody well before you try to sing the additional verses. You may have to change the rhythm slightly to fit the melody. For example, the eighth note pickups in measures 4, 8, and 12 will become one quarter note in some of the verses.

STEWBALL

2. I rode him in England
   I rode him in Spain,
   And I never did lose, boys,
   I always did gain.

3. So come all you gamblers,
   From near and from far,
   Don't bet your gold dollar
   On that little gray mare.

4. Most likely she'll stumble,
   Most likely she'll fall,
   But you never will lose, boys
   On my noble Stewball.

5. Sit tight in your saddle,
   Let slack on your rein,
   And you never will lose, boys,
   You always will gain.

Practice the basic alternating bass note/strum pattern and two other strum patterns.
After you can play them well, play "Stewball" and use one of the patterns.

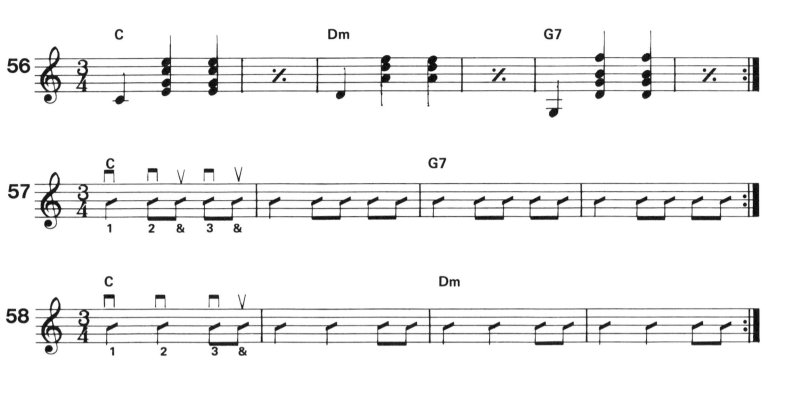

The following exercises are variations of the basic bass note/strum pattern. Instead of playing the same note all the way through a song, vary the bass note on each chord. After practicing these two exercises, go back and play this pattern as you sing the melody.

Now you are ready to play an instrumental version which uses several of the ideas you have been practicing. Folk singers will often use an instrumental solo like this between verses of a song.

STEWBALL

HOLD DOWN THE CHORD

LICKS

When a song has a held note in the melody, a player will often improvise his own material during that time. This is called many things: a lick, fill, riff, break, ride. One example is shown below and could be used in measures 3 and 15 in "Stewball." Create your own licks to fill measures 6-8 and 11 and 12.

You are now ready to play WILDWOOD FLOWER, pg. 13 of Hal Leonard's MORE EASY POP MELODIES.

The A Minor Scale

You know the pattern of whole-steps and half-steps for a major scale. By changing the combination of whole and half-steps we can build new scales. If we begin a scale on the note A and use the pattern shown, an A minor scale is created.

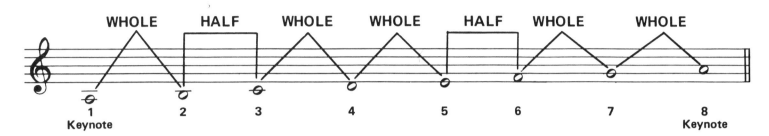

Notice that there is a half-step between notes 2 and 3 and again between 5 and 6. Practice the A minor scale and listen carefully.

Two songs can have the same key signature but be in different keys. They have different keynotes. Play the two versions of "Frere Jacques." Exercise 64 is in the key of C Major and has no sharps or flats in the key signature. Exercise 65 is in A minor and also has a key signature of no sharps or flats.

FRERE JACQUES

FRERE JACQUES

Did you notice the difference between the two songs? This difference in sound is caused by the changing of the whole and half-step pattern.

Practice the following exercise which is written in A minor. Remember there are no sharps or flats in the key signature.

WAYFARING STRANGER

I'm just a poor_____ way - far - ing stran - ger,_____ Trav - 'ling through_____ this world of woe._____ But there's no sick - ness_____ no toil or dan - ger,_____ in that bright land_____ to which I go._____ I'm go - ing there_____ to see my fa - ther,_____ I'm go - ing there_____ no more to roam._____ I'm just a - go - ing o - ver Jor - dan,_____ I'm just a - go - ing o - ver home._____

After you can play the melody well, practice the chords. An effective accompaniment for this song would be the alternating bass note/chord rhythm shown in Exercise 67.

In this song the melody is in the top notes of the chords. Practice the melody only before adding the chords. The tempo of this piece should be flexible.

BLACK IS THE COLOR OF MY TRUE LOVE'S HAIR

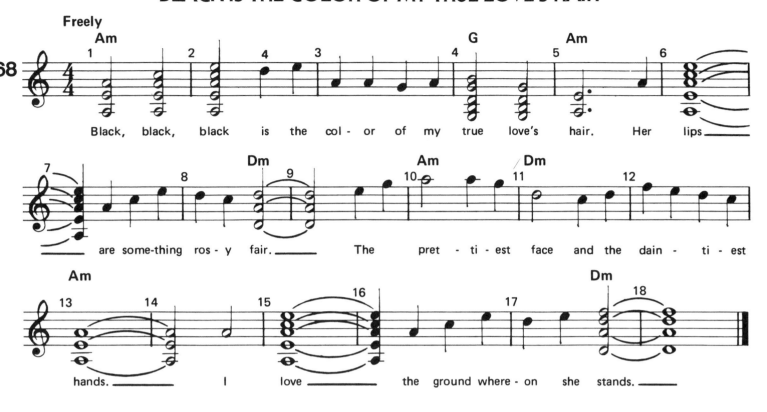

Black, black, black is the col-or of my true love's hair. Her lips are some-thing ros-y fair. The pret-ti-est face and the dain-ti-est hands. I love the ground where-on she stands.

Practice the following song slowly and steadily; then gradually increase the tempo. You may want to use Variation I or II as a strumming accompaniment to this piece.

BOUND FOR THE PROMISED LAND

You are now ready to play SIXTEEN TONS, pg. 14 of Hal Leonard's MORE EASY POP MELODIES.

The E Chord

The E chord uses the same finger position as the Am chord but is played on strings three, four, and five. The bass string for the E chord is the open sixth string.

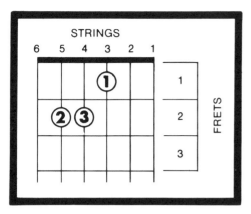

The Harmonic Minor Scale

There are different types of minor scales. On page 29 you learned the whole and half-step pattern for an A natural minor scale. The A harmonic minor has the following pattern:

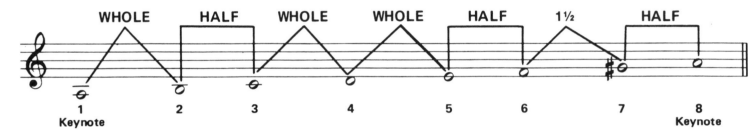

| WHOLE | HALF | WHOLE | WHOLE | HALF | 1½ | HALF |

1 Keynote 2 3 4 5 6 7 8 Keynote

Look at the diagram for the fingering of G♯; then practice the A harmonic minor scale shown above.

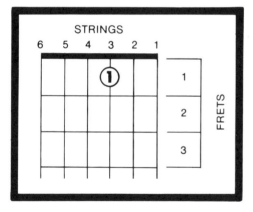

Exercise 70 uses the A harmonic minor scale.

JOSHUA FOUGHT THE BATTLE OF JERICHO

Josh-ua fought the bat-tle of ___ Jer-i-cho, ___ Jer-i-cho, ___ Jer-i-cho, _____

Josh-ua fought the bat-tle of ___ Jer-i-cho, ___ And the walls came tum-bling down!

You are now ready to play FOLSOM PRISON BLUES, pg. 15 of Hal Leonard's MORE EASY POP MELODIES.

One of the best known songs written in the harmonic minor is the Israeli dance, "Hava Nagila." Traditionally you should begin this song at a slow tempo and gradually increase the speed as you complete it. Remember that a sharp affects all notes on that line or space in one measure.

HAVA NAGILA

You are now ready to play CAN'T BUY ME LOVE, pg. 16 of Hal Leonard's MORE EASY POP MELODIES.

12-Bar Blues

The traditional form of Blues has twelve measures or bars with a particular pattern of chords. These chords are based on a major scale. Another characteristic of blues is the playing or singing of blues notes, notes that are one half-step lower than the scale note. The following diagram shows the E blues scale. It is similar to a major scale except that the third and seventh are lowered one half-step.

The B7 Chord

Study the finger position for the B7 chord. Because E is a traditional blues key for guitar, you will need to know this chord to play the blues. The bass note for the B7 chord is the fifth string.

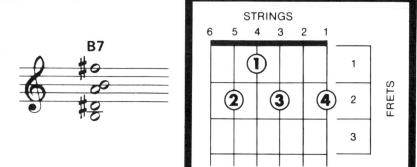

Practice the melody line; then strum the chords. Vocalists often use syllables to fill in words they have forgotten or to imitate the sounds of the instruments. This is called scat singing. In Exercise 73 syllables have already been added for you to sing as you strum the chords. You can also create your own.

THE BLUES

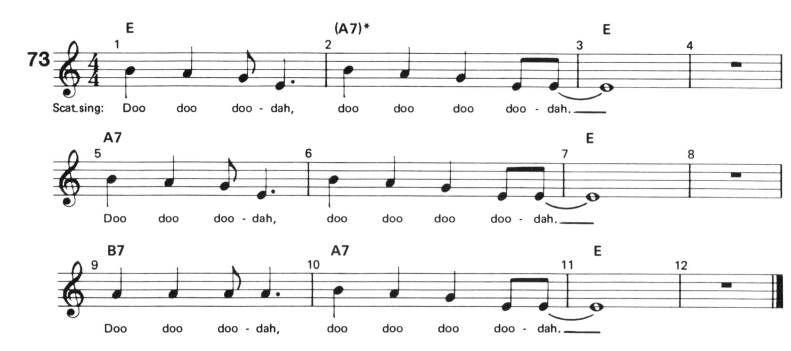

Scat sing: Doo doo doo - dah, doo doo doo doo - dah. ___

*The A7 chord in measure 2 is an optional chord. Play either E or A7 in this measure.

You are now ready to play STEAM ROLLER BLUES, pg. 17 of Hal Leonard's MORE EASY POP MELODIES.

New Note B♭ or A♯

Between the notes A and B there is one whole-step or two half-steps. As you know, a **sharp** (♯) **raises** the pitch of a note one half-step. A♯ is the third fret of the third string, one half-step above A.

If you would play B on the third string rather than the open second string, it would be the fourth fret. As you know, a **flat** (♭) **lowers** the pitch of a note one half-step. B♭ would then be the third fret of the third string, one half-step below B.

Since both A♯ and B♭ are on the third fret of the third string and sound the same, they are called enharmonic tones. Usually the A♯ is written when the melody is ascending and the B♭ is written when the melody is descending.

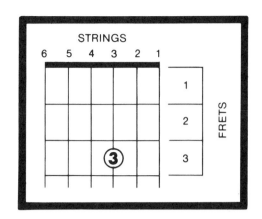

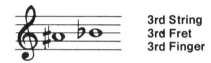

3rd String
3rd Fret
3rd Finger

Practice the melody of Exercise 74; then sing as you play the chord accompaniment. Experiment with the strum patterns you know to find one that fits with the melody.

24-HOUR BLUES

I got the blues in the morn-in' and the blues all thru the night.___

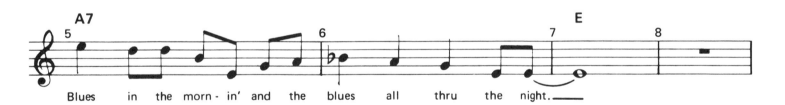

Blues in the morn - in' and the blues all thru the night.___

Lov - in' you ba - by's the on-ly thing gon - na put me right. ___

When you played "Stewball," you added a lick or fill to give the song variety. You can also add licks to blues when a note is held or there is a rest. The following examples could be used to fill measures 3 and 4 and measures 7 and 8 in Exercise 74.

TYPICAL BLUES "LICKS"

C♯

Check the fingering for C♯ before you play Exercise 75.

Rock is another style of popular music. Exercise 75 is a typical Blues-Rock bass line that you have heard in many songs. After practicing it several times, sing the "24-Hour Blues" melody above it. Start the guitar part on the first beat of measure 1 in the "24-Hour Blues."

5th STRING
4th FRET
4th FINGER

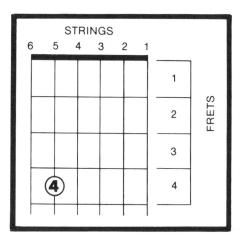

BLUES-ROCK BASS

Here's another blues song in the key of G. Remember that a blues scale is like a major scale with a lowered third and fifth. You may want to improvise your own licks in measures 7 and 8. In measure 4 there is a new symbol, a natural sign, ♮. A natural sign cancels a sharp or flat on that line or space for that measure.

You are now ready to play SHAKE, RATTLE AND ROLL, pg. 18 of Hal Leonard's MORE EASY POP MELODIES.

The E Minor Scale

The key signature of E minor is one sharp (♯). Practice the scale until you are familiar with the fingering patterns.

Play the melody and then sing as you play the chordal accompaniment.

ALL THE PRETTY LITTLE HORSES

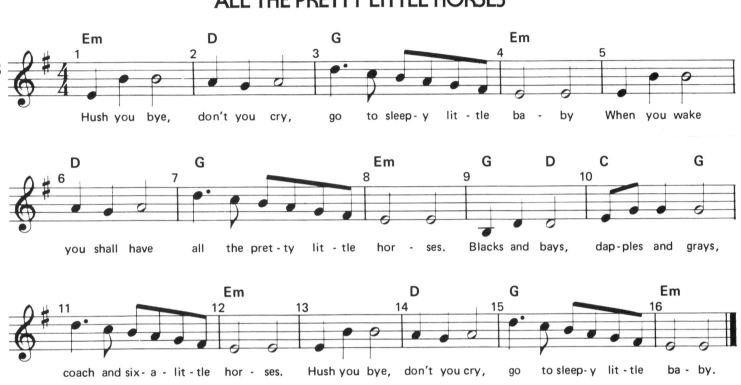

Hush you bye, don't you cry, go to sleep-y lit-tle ba-by When you wake

you shall have all the pret-ty lit-tle hor-ses. Blacks and bays, dap-ples and grays,

coach and six-a-lit-tle hor-ses. Hush you bye, don't you cry, go to sleep-y lit-tle ba-by.

Playing Arpeggios

When a chord is played one note at a time rather than simultaneously, it is called an arpeggio. These arpeggios can be played ascending or descending. Practice Exercises 79 and 80 and then sing the melody of "All The Pretty Little Horses" above these ascending arpeggios. Be sure to study the chord pattern and play the correct chord where indicated.

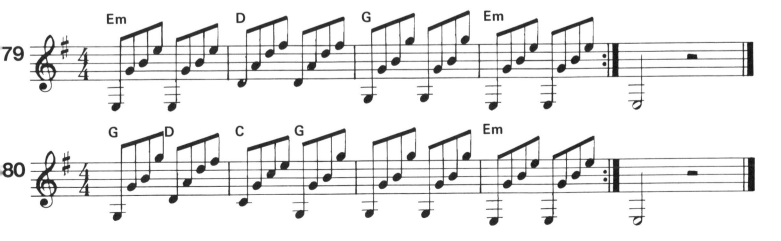

The E Harmonic Minor

THREE F#s

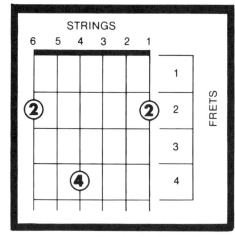

TWO D#s

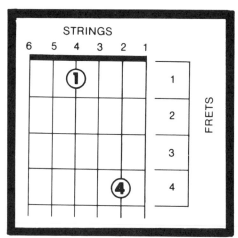

Check the fingerings for the new notes shown above.

Remember that the harmonic minor has a raised seventh step. In E minor, this note would be D#. Practice the harmonic minor scale below in two octaves.

The melody of Exercise 82 is built upon both the E natural minor and E harmonic minor scales. Practice the melody until you can play it easily and steadily; then sing the melody as you strum the chords. You can also play an alternating bass note/ chord strum accompaniment as you sing.

KEEP YOUR HAND ON THE PLOW

Paul and Si - las bound in jail, had no mon - ey for their bail, Keep your hand on - a the

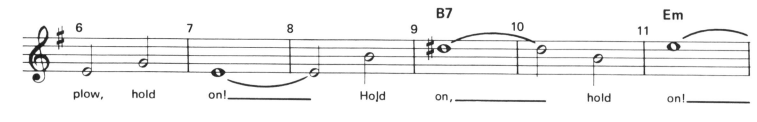

plow, hold on! _____ Hold on, _____ hold on! _____

_____ Keep your hand on - a the plow, hold on. _____

You are now ready to play A DAY IN THE LIFE OF A FOOL, pg. 20 of Hal Leonard's MORE EASY POP MELODIES.

Bass Runs

You've already learned to improvise licks or fills when there is a held note in the melody. You can also add variety to your bass lines by adding a bass run similar to a lick or fill. In Exercise 83 there is a very easy bass run from G to C in measure 4 and from C to G in measure 8.

Watch the alternating bass notes on the chords. The alternate bass note on the C chord in this exercise can be played by moving only the third finger to the sixth string, third fret, to play low G. Play slowly at first; then gradually increase the tempo.

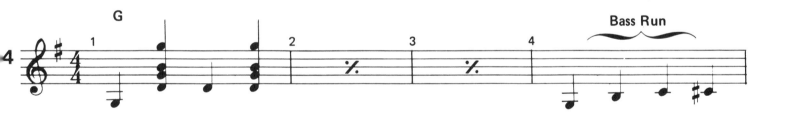

In Exercise 84 the bass run moves from G to D in measure 4 and from D to G in measure 8. To add variety a C♯ is added to the run and creates a half-step pattern (B-C-C♯-D). This movement by half steps is called **chromatic**. Remember that C♯ is played with the fourth finger on the fifth string. Don't slide your fingers. Use a different finger for each note.

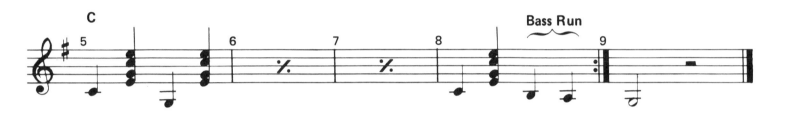

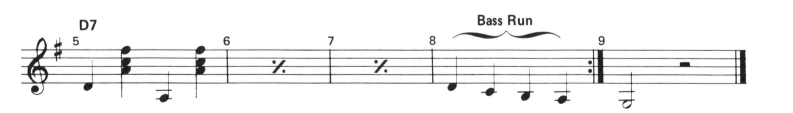

Bluegrass Music

Bluegrass music is a style of instrumental music which grew out of traditional Appalachian folk music, Anglo-American fiddle tunes, and blues-influenced banjo playing. It is named after Bill Monroe's band, The Blue Grass Boys. Bill Monroe is often called the father of bluegrass music and members of this band included the well-known artists Lester Flatt and Earl Scruggs. One typical bluegrass-style song is "The Banks Of The Ohio."

BANKS OF THE OHIO

You are now ready to play DADDY SANG BASS, pg. 21 of Hal Leonard's MORE EASY POP MELODIES.

One of the best known bluegrass songs is "Roll In My Sweet Baby's Arms." The melody is the same for the verse and the chorus. It is an easy melody to harmonize, and after you learn it, you can play it at a fast tempo. Remember that you may have to change the rhythm to fit the words of the verse. The first syllable on the first beat of each measure is underlined. After you can play the melody and play the guitar part at a slow speed, begin to increase the tempo gradually.

ROLL IN MY SWEET BABY'S ARMS

1. <u>Ain't</u> gonna work on the <u>rail</u>road,
   <u>Ain't</u> gonna work on the <u>farm</u>.
   Gonna <u>lay</u> 'round the shack till the <u>mail</u> train comes back,
   Then I'll <u>roll</u> in my sweet baby's <u>arms</u>.   CHORUS.

2. They <u>tell</u> me your parents don't <u>like</u> me;
   They <u>drove</u> me away from your <u>door</u>;
   If <u>I</u> had my life to live <u>over</u>,
   I'd <u>never</u> go there any <u>more</u>.   CHORUS.

The F Major Scale

The key of F has one flat (B♭) in the key signature. The half-steps should fall between steps 3 and 4 and again between 7 and 8 in the F major scale. Practice the scale slowly and carefully; then gradually increase the speed. Remember B♭ is played with the third finger on the third fret of the third string.

In Exercise 88 you'll be using a new fingering on some of the G's. In measure 4 and 7 the G is preceded by B♭. You shouldn't slide your third finger over to the first string so play the G with the fourth finger.

THE GOLDEN VANITY

Remember the notes that are not normally a part of the scale are called accidentals, like the C# in measures 10, 11, and 12.

THE MINSTREL BOY

Here's another song in the key of F major. Notice the natural sign on B in measure 15.

THE ASH GROVE

You are now ready to play CANDLE ON THE WATER, pg. 22 of Hal Leonard's MORE EASY POP MELODIES.

$\frac{6}{8}$ Time

Until now you have played time signatures in which the quarter note received one beat. In $\frac{6}{8}$ time the bottom number tells you that the eighth note now gets one beat and the top number tells you that there are six beats in one measure. Practice this new time signature in Exercise 91.

IRISH WASHER WOMAN

In $\frac{6}{8}$ time all note and rest values are proportionate to the eighth note.

| 1 BEAT | 2 BEATS | 3 BEATS |

When $\frac{6}{8}$ is played at a faster tempo, you will feel a definite grouping of two. Each group of two has three eighth notes so the strong beats of the measure are 1 and 4. Practice Exercise 92 slowly at first. After you know the melody and the fingering patterns, increase the speed and think of two groups per measure.

PATSY-ORY-ORY-AYE

You are now ready to play HOPELESSLY DEVOTED TO YOU, pg. 24 of Hal Leonard's MORE EASY POP MELODIES.

Here's another song in $\frac{6}{8}$ time. Practice it slowly at first; then increase the tempo so you feel two beat groups per measure. When you are strumming the chords, strum two in each measure on beats 1 and 4.

WEE COOPER O'FIFE

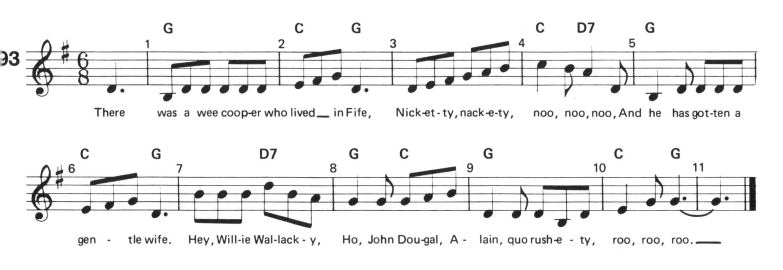

There was a wee coop-er who lived __ in Fife, Nick-et-ty, nack-e-ty, noo, noo, noo, And he has got-ten a

gen - tle wife. Hey, Will-ie Wal-lack-y, Ho, John Dou-gal, A - lain, quo rush-e - ty, roo, roo, roo. __

$\frac{9}{8}$ Time

A $\frac{9}{8}$ time signature is similar to the $\frac{6}{8}$ time signature because the eighth note gets one beat. In $\frac{9}{8}$ there are nine beats to a measure. The eighth notes are grouped in threes, three groups per measure.

JESU, JOY OF MAN'S DESIRING

Another Look At Old Chords

To complete the second book a beautiful arrangement of "Plasir D'Amour" has been written. It combines melody and chords and the melody is in the top notes. There are several partial chords and some modified chords. Always finger the complete chords and strum only the notes notated.

G/B CHORD

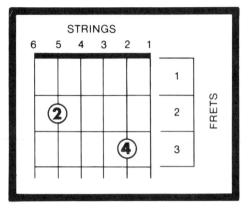 

The first modified chord you have is in measure 2. It is a G chord with the note B in the bass and is notated G/B. Look at the fingering illustration and then strum the chord.

MODIFIED G7 CHORD

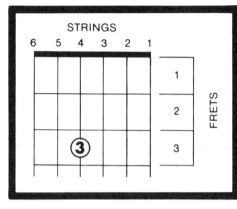 

The other modified chord is a G7. It uses strings 2, 3, and 4. Study the illustration and try strumming the chord before you play this song.

Remember to play the melody (top notes only) before you combine the melody and the chords.

PLAISIR D'AMOUR

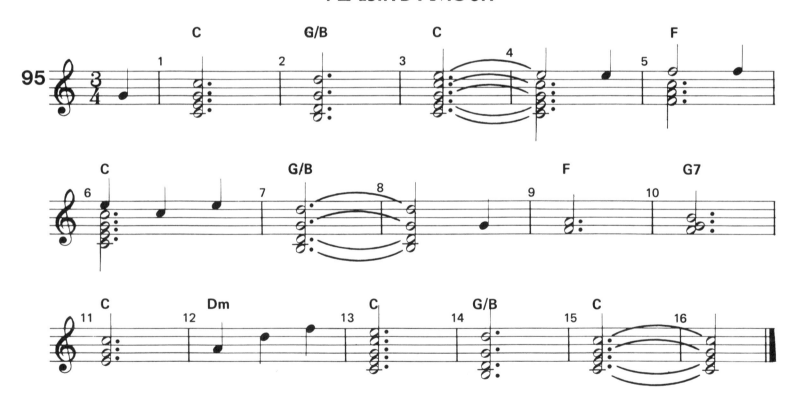

Chord Chart

In this chart you will find all of the chords you learned in this book. There are also several of the more common chords you may see in other music you are playing.

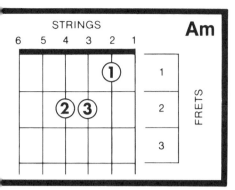

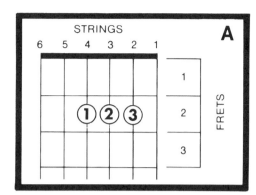

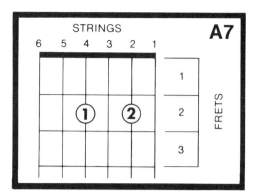

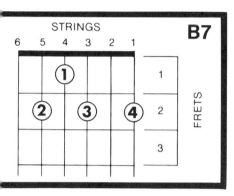

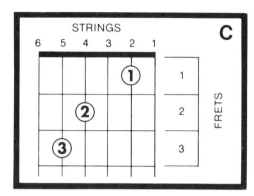

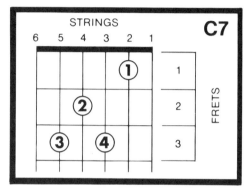

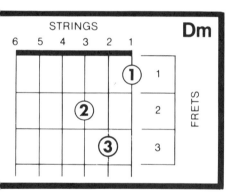

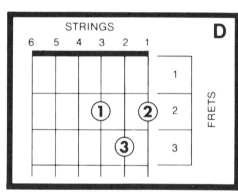

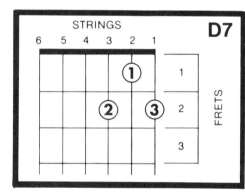

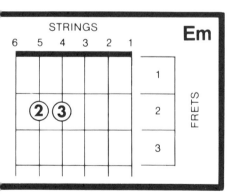

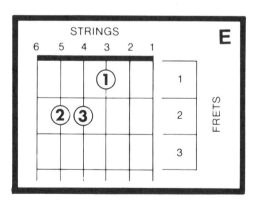

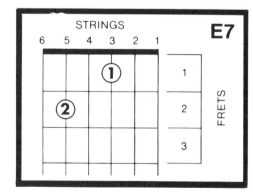

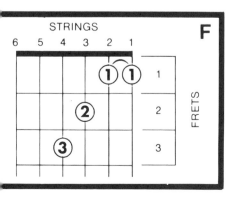

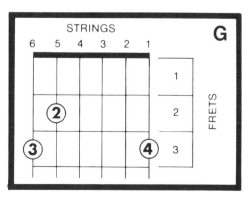

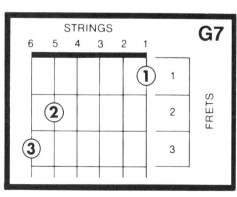

THE HAL LEONARD GUITAR METHOD

MORE THAN A METHOD ...IT'S A SYSTEM.

This comprehensive method is preferred by teachers and students alike for many reasons:

- Learning Sequence is carefully paced with clear instructions that make it easy to learn
- Popular Songs increase the incentive to learn to play
- Versatile enough to be used as self-instruction or with a teacher
- Audio accompaniments let students have fun and sound great while practicing.

HAL LEONARD METHOD BOOK 1
Features great songs and provides beginning instruction which includes tuning, 1st position melody playing, chords, rhythms through eighth notes, solos and ensembles, and strumming. Also includes a handy chord chart. Pages are cross referenced for use with supplements.

00699010 Book..$4.95
00699026 Book/Cassette Pack $12.95
00699027 Book/CD Pack.............................$14.95

HAL LEONARD METHOD BOOK 2
Book 2 includes studies and songs in the keys of C, G, D, Em, and F, syncopations and dotted rhythms, more advanced strums, the most common 1st position chords, solos, bass runs, and a variety of styles from bluegrass to blues-rock. A great selection of traditional songs, including "Simple Gifts," "Mamma Don't Low," "Roll In My Sweet Baby's Arms," "Jesu, Joy Of Man's Desiring," and many more. Pages are cross-referenced for supplements.
00699020 ....$4.95

HAL LEONARD METHOD BOOK 3
Book 3 includes the chromatic scale, 16th notes, playing in positions II-IIV, moving chords up the neck (bar chords), finger picking, ensembles and solos, a wide variety of style studies and many excellent songs for playing and/or singing. Can be used with supplements.
00699030 ....$4.95

COMPOSITE
Books 1, 2 and 3 bound together in an easy-to-use comb binding.
00699040 ....$12.95

GUITAR METHOD SUPPLEMENTS
These unique books will work with *any* Guitar Method Books 1, 2, or 3. The play-along cassettes and CDs feature guitar on the left channel and full rhythm section on the right. Each book is filled with great pop songs!

EASY POP MELODIES
A unique pop supplement to any guitar method book 1. Cross-referenced with Book 1 pages for easy student and teacher use. Featured songs: Feelings • Let It Be • Every Breath You Take • You Needed Me • Heartbreak Hotel.

00699150 Book..$4.95
00699148 Book/Cassette Pack.....................$12.95
00697268 Book/CD Pack.............................$14.95

MORE EASY POP MELODIES
A unique pop supplement to any guitar method book 2. Cross-referenced with pages for easy student and teacher use. Featured songs: Long And Winding Road • Say, Say, Say • King Of Pain • and more.

00699151 Book..$4.95
00699149 Book/Cassette Pack.....................$12.95
00697269 Book/CD Pack.............................$14.95

POP MELODIES PLUS
Pop supplement cross-referenced to guitar book 3. Features: Cool Change • Daniel • Memory • Maneater • and many more.

00699154 Book..$4.95
00699156 Book/Cassette Pack...................$12.95
00699155 Cassette......................................$8.95
00697270 Book/CD Pack.............................$14.95

ROCK TRAX 1
This book is a suppleme to ANY Method Book 1. also teaches rhythm guit lead guitar and solo lick The exciting play-alo cassette features a gre sounding rhythm section a demonstrates each exerci in the book. Rock Trax unique because it provid the teacher with a program to teach rock guit technique when the student begins lessons.
00699165 Book/Cassette Pack....................$12.9
00697271 Book/CD Pack.............................$14.9

ROCK TRAX 2
This rock guitar suppleme to any Method Book teaches rhythm guitar, le improvisation, and solo lick The tape provides eig background rhythm trac and demonstrates both t solo licks and new ro guitar techniques. Includ music and tablature.
00699167 Book/Cassette Pack....................$12.9
00697272 Book CD/Pack.............................$14.9

ROCK HITS FOR 1, 2 OR 3 GUITARS
Supplement to any Meth Books 1 and 2. The arrangements are playable 1, 2, or 3 guitars class/ensemble. The ta features lead, harmony a rhythm guitar parts with ba backup on Side A. Side repeats the complete ba accompaniments without guitar parts 1 or "Practice Notes" aid the student and teacher w each song being ideal for lessons, recitals or a home enjoyment. Contents: Sister Christian • Ro Around The Clock • Johnny B. Goode • Rocket M • Sad Songs (Say So Much) • Hungry Like The W • Maggie May.
00699168 Book/Cassette Pack....................$12.9
00697273 Book/CD Pack.............................$14.9

INCREDIBLE CHORD FINDE
A complete guide di gramming over 1,000 guit chords in their most comme voicings. It is arrang chromatically and each cho is illustrated in three ways f three levels of difficulty. No names of each string a indicated on each cho diagram to let the player know what notes are bei played in the chord.
00697208 ....$5.9

BEGINNING GUITAR VIDEO
This video, especially cross-re erenced with the Hal Leona Guitar Method Book 1 and its su plements, Easy Pop Melodies a Rock Trax, teaches: • How to pl chords • How to read music • Ho to play solos and duets • How improvise rock • How to accom any singing in wide variety musical styles.
It's hosted by Will Schmid, one of the world leading guitar teachers and authors, and featur such great songs as "Every Breath You Take," "M Of Kintrye" and more. On-screen music, guit diagrams, playing tips with close-up hand positio and demonstrations make for easy learning. Al includes Play-along Trax with full ba accompaniment. 60 minutes.
00730627 ....$29.9

Hal Leonard GUITAR METHOD ™

by Will Schmid

Will Schmid has gained the reputation as an outstanding guitar teacher and performer throughout the United States. He received his BA from Luther College and his PhD from the Eastman School of Music. While teaching at the University of Kansas, he created and performed a series of programs entitled "Folk Music Americana" for National Public Radio. He is currently Associate Professor of Music Education at the University of Wisconsin-Milwaukee. During the summer of 1976-1977 he was a guest lecturer at the Eastman School of Music and taught classes including a guitar workshop.

Contents

The Chromatic Scale. 2
  Arkansas Traveler 5
  Miss McCloud's Reel. 6
  Soldier's Joy. 6
  I Was Born About 10,000 Years Ago 7
  Goober Peas 8
  Tramp, Tramp, Tramp. 8
  Roller Coaster Waltz 9
Moving Up The Neck 10
Position II—A Major 10
  Sweet Betsy From Pike 11
  The Devil's Dream. 11
Position II—D Major 12
  The Water Is Wide 12-13
Position V—C Major 14
  Joy To The World. 15
  Barbara Allen. 15
  Deep River. 15
Shifting Positions 16
  Shifty. 18
Finger Picking. 19
  He's Got The Whole World In His Hands 20

Rock-A-My Soul. 20
Man Of Constant Sorrow 21
Moving Chords Up The Neck 22
Position V—F Major 28
  I Saw Three Ships 28
Position IV—E Major. 29
  Hush, Little Baby. 29
Position V—D minor 30
  Greensleeves. 30
  Sore Finger Rock 32
  Hey, Guitar Man. 33
  Stardom Variations 34
Studies In Thirds. 36
  Going Latin. 37
  Shifting Into Third 38
  All My Trials 39
  The Brazos 40
  The Butcher Boy 42-43
Position VII—D Major 44
  Flow Gently, Sweet Afton. 44
Chord Chart 46

HAL•LEONARD ™ CORPORATION

7777 W. BLUEMOUND RD. P.O. BOX 13819 MILWAUKEE, WI 53213

The Chromatic Scale

You know that each fret on the guitar represents one half-step and that scales have a particular pattern of whole and half-steps. When the scale pattern is made entirely of half-steps, it is called a **chromatic scale**. You'll notice in the diagram below that there are several enharmonic tones, tones that sound the same but have different letter names. In a chromatic scale or melody the note with the sharp sign is usually used in an ascending line. When the melody or scale is descending, the note with the flat sign is used.

Study the positions shown below and then practice the chromatic scale.

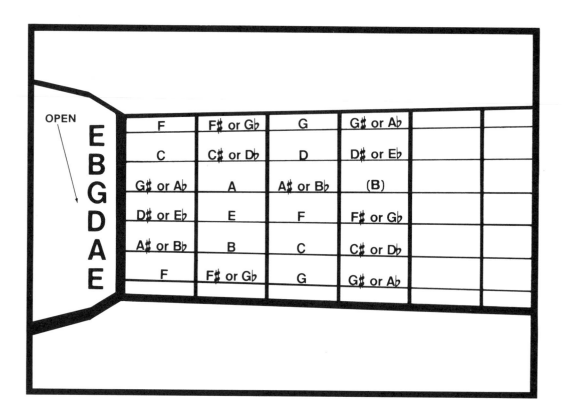

THE CHROMATIC SCALE

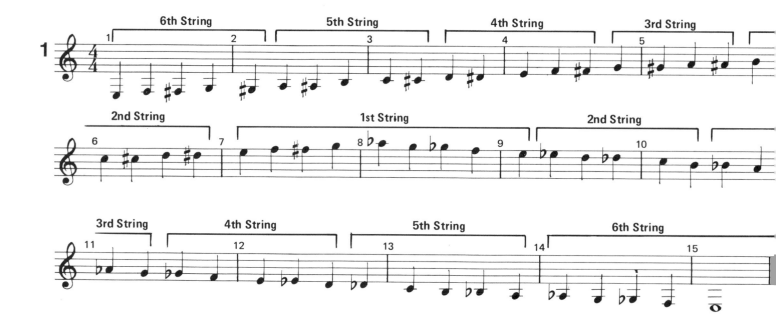

2

Practice each of the exercises until you can play them well. Begin slowly at first and gradually increase the speed.

CHROMATIC EXERCISE

CHROMATIC BLUES

Sixteenth Notes

A note that receives ¼ beat is called a **sixteenth note** and has two flags or a double beam ♪ 𝅘𝅥𝅯𝅘𝅥𝅯𝅘𝅥𝅯𝅘𝅥𝅯 .

The following chart shows how each type of note can be subdivided.

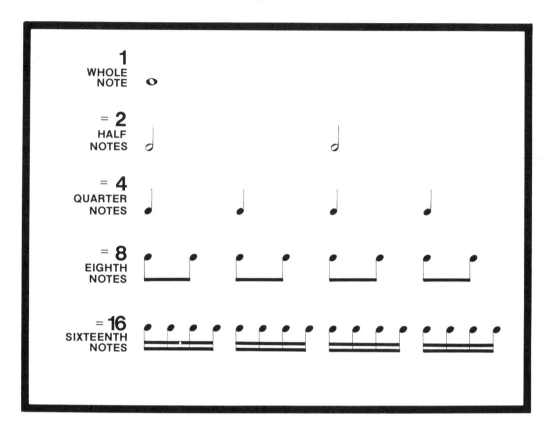

Since there are four sixteenth notes in one quarter note beat, count them by adding the syllable "a" (pronounced "uh"). The counting would be:

Practice the following sixteenth note exercises. Begin playing them slowly and accurately, then increase the tempo. Tap your foot on each beat of the measure.

4

2/4 Time

Remember that the top number of a time signature tells you how many beats are in one measure. In 2/4 time there are two beats in a measure and a quarter note gets one beat.

One of the best ways to develop fast, steady sixteenth note technique is to practice traditional bluegrass fiddle tunes. A primary characteristic of these tunes is that the melody is embellished with sixteenths. In the following duet, part 1 is the melody and part 2 is the duet part. Practice both parts until you can play them smoothly. Start slowly at first; then gradually increase the tempo. Ask your teacher or a friend to play the duet. If you have a tape recorder, you can record one part and play a duet with yourself.

ARKANSAS TRAVELER

Here are two more fiddle tunes. A reel is a type of dance which originated in Scotland or Ireland. This particular melody was used as a part of Aaron Copland's composition, **Rodeo**.

Practice the melody slowly at first; then gradually increase the speed as you learn the fingering and picking patterns. After you know the melody play a bass note/afterbeat accompaniment part like part 2 of "Arkansas Traveler."

MISS McCLOUD'S REEL

Hold down the C chord when there is a bracket indicated. This will help you because your fingers will be in the correct position.

SOLDIER'S JOY

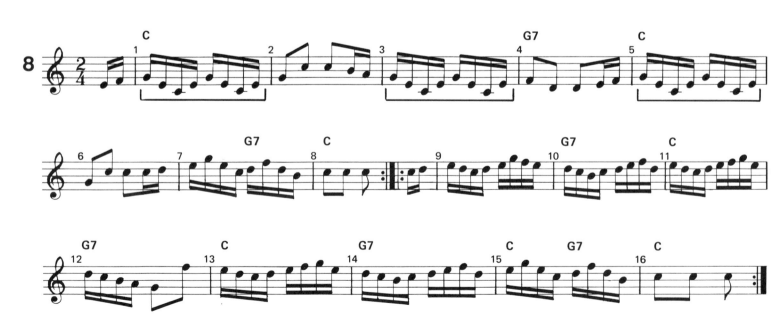

Dotted Eighth Notes

Like the other dotted notes you've played, the dot after an eighth note increases the value of the note by one-half.

Since the dotted eighth receives only a part of a beat in $\frac{4}{4}$, $\frac{3}{4}$, or $\frac{2}{4}$ time, a sixteenth is added to it to complete the beat.

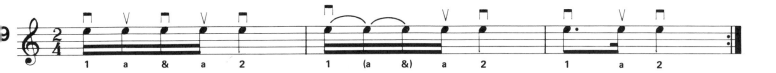

An easy way to learn a dotted eighth is to think of it as three tied sixteenth notes. This will help you play the rhythm more accurately. Practice the following exercise until you can play the subdivision of the beat easily.

Before playing the following exercise, speak the words out loud in their correct rhythm.

I WAS BORN ABOUT 10,000 YEARS AGO

On the next pages you will be playing several exercises which use the dotted eighth/sixteenth note pattern. Practice each carefully until you feel comfortable with this rhythm.

Common Time

The symbol **C** is another way of writing $\frac{4}{4}$ time and stands for "common time."
Remember that there are four beats in a measure and a quarter note gets one beat.

GOOBER PEAS

Always look at the key signature before you begin to play a song.

TRAMP, TRAMP, TRAMP

The Key of A Major

Study the key signature for A Major, F♯, C♯, and G♯, before you begin playing Exercise 13. Locate all of the G♯'s on your fingerboard and review the correct fingering.

The fingering pattern for the four highest notes of the A major scale is special. Play F♯ with the first finger and G♯ with the third finger. This is different from the way you learned it originally and should be used in the key of A.

A MAJOR SCALE STUDY

Practice all of the exercises until you can play them easily. If any measures seem difficult, isolate those measures and practice them slowly. As you learn the fingering patterns, gradually increase the tempo.

ROLLER COASTER WALTZ

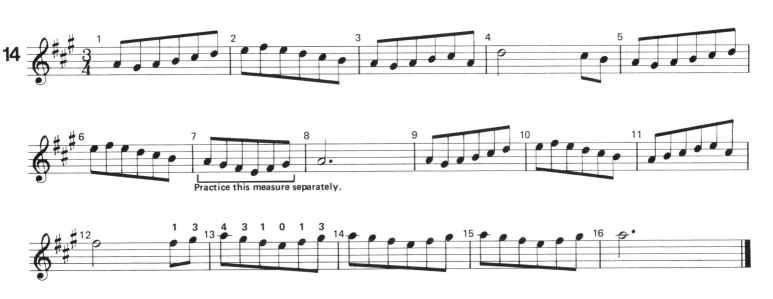

Practice this measure separately.

Moving Up The Neck

Unlike many other instruments that have only one key or one fingering for each note, the guitar allows you to play the same pitch in a number of different positions. For example the notes B and F may be played in the positions shown below.

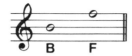

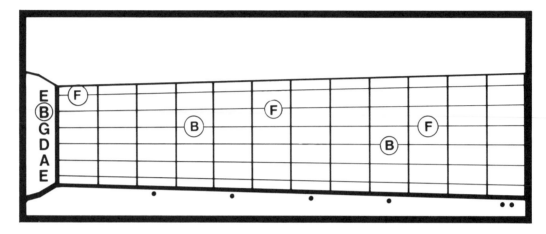

Moving notes to different places on the neck is called **position playing**. The position (place on the neck) is numbered for the fret on which you have your first finger. In Position II your first finger is on fret 2, Position V begins with your finger on the fifth fret, and so on.

Choosing the best way to finger a melody is one of the primary challenges to the advancing guitarist. The first step in your development will be to explore the possibilities of Position II.

Position II — A Major

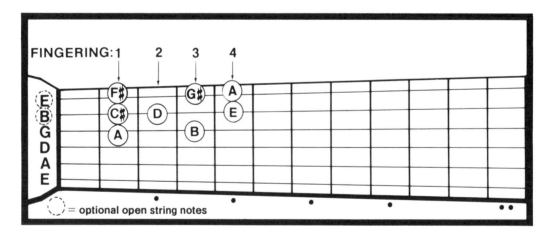

= optional open string notes

Watch your fingering carefully as you play the A Major scale below. Be sure to practice both sets of fingerings.

Play Exercise 16 completely in Position II. When a finger roll is indicated between A and C♯ and between E and A, simply flatten the finger so that it depresses both notes without lifting the tip of the finger.

SWEET BETSY FROM PIKE

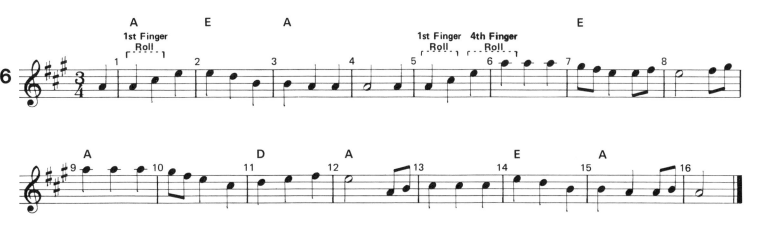

The fiddle tune, "Devil's Dream," will give you a good opportunity to practice both second position, A Major, and the down/up pick stroke on sixteenth notes. Practice the song slowly until you have learned the fingering patterns.

Watch the fingerings indicated above the notes because there are some that are different from the fingerings you originally learned. The music will be easier to play if you use these fingerings. When there is a bracket under a series of notes, hold all the fingers down as you would in playing a chord.

THE DEVIL'S DREAM

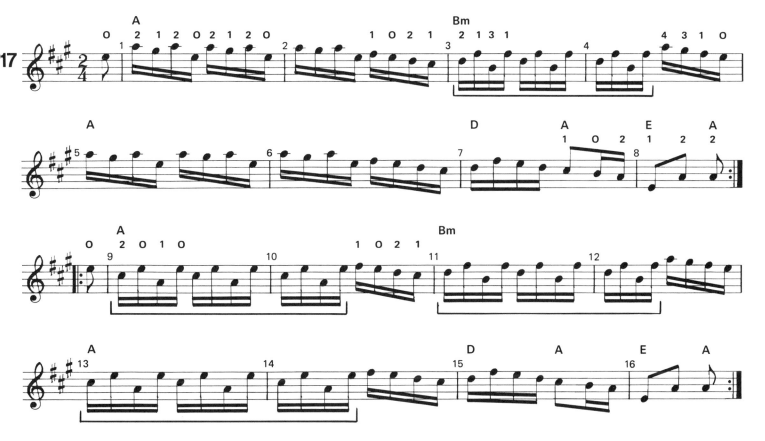

Position II—D Major

Now try the key of D Major in Position II. Remember that your first finger will be on the second fret. The fingerings shown below the staff are optional fingerings using open strings. Practice the scale study using both sets of fingerings. After you can play it with either finger position, choose the one that is best for the music you are playing.

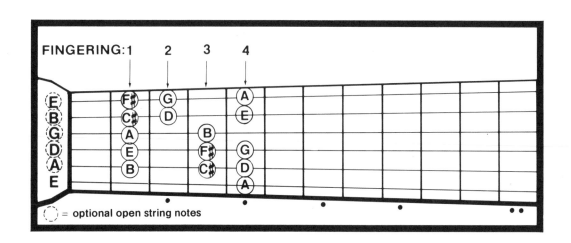

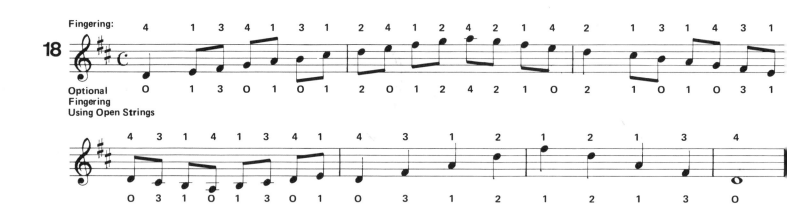

Use only Position II in Exercise 19.

THE WATER IS WIDE

In this book you'll be learning a number of new chords. Instead of a separate diagram like you saw in Book 1 and 2, a chord diagram will be shown in the music where the new chord occurs. Before playing the song, look at the finger positions for the chords and strum them several times. The new chords in measure 5 and measure 9 begin on frets higher on the neck. Use the position shown and move your hand to the fret indicated.

After you can play the music easily and know the melody well, sing the verses as you play.

THE WATER IS WIDE

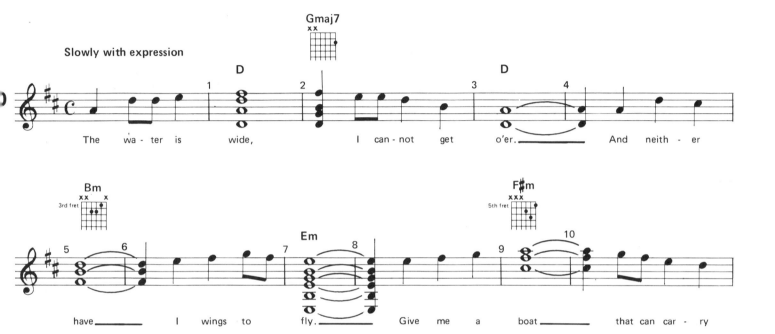

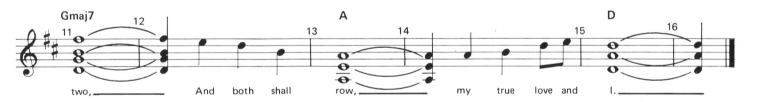

2. Oh, love is <u>hand</u>some and love is <u>fine</u>,
   Bright as a <u>jew</u>el when it is <u>new</u>,
   But love grows <u>old</u>, and waxes <u>cold</u>,
   And fades a<u>way</u> like morning <u>dew</u>.

Position V—C Major

Now try the key of C Major in Position V (first finger on the fifth fret). Once you have learned the fingering pattern for this scale well, you will be able to play many other scales by simply moving to another position.

The C on the first string, eighth fret, looks like this:

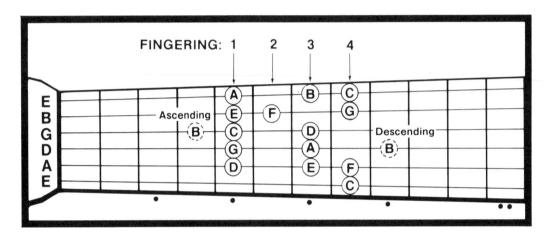

When you go up the scale, you usually play B on the third string, fourth fret and slide your finger to C on the fifth fret. To play a descending scale, play B on the fourth string, ninth fret. You will have to stretch your fourth finger to the ninth fret to play this B. Study the music and try both ways to decide which fingering is best.

When a roll is indicated, flatten your finger so it depresses all notes at one time.

Play the following songs in Position V.

JOY TO THE WORLD

BARBARA ALLEN

DEEP RIVER

Shifting Positions I—V

When you are moving from Position I to Position V, the movement is called **shifting**. There are a number of accepted ways of shifting, but the important thing is to accomplish it with a smooth, connected sound.

The following general rules will help you learn to shift positions easily and clearly.

1. The thumb should stay in a position roughly between fingers one and two.

2. During the shift, maintain the normal hand and finger position to assure the correct placement of the fingers in the new position.

3. When you are shifting, the **leading finger** should maintain pressure on the string until the **following finger** is in its new position. On an ascending line the **3rd** or **4th** finger is the **leading finger**. The **1st** finger is the **leading finger** on a descending melody. When ascending, the **following** finger is the 1st and when descending, it is the 3rd or 4th.

4. The **following finger** should slide along the string until its new position is reached. The **leading finger** releases its pressure just as the following finger plays its first note in the new position.

5. The shift should be made as quickly as possible.

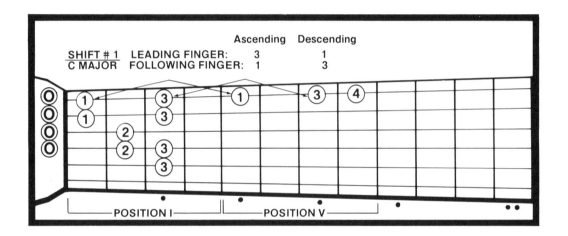

Practice the C Major scale with this shift.

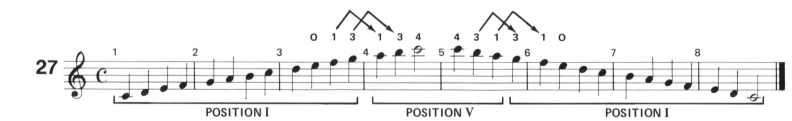

16

Now practice shifting on the second string.

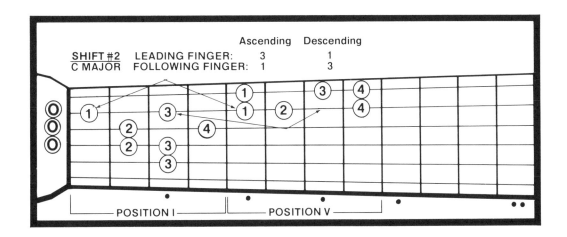

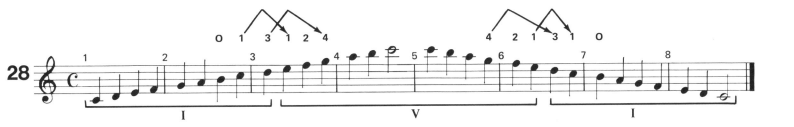

In this pattern the 4th finger is used as the **leading finger** on the ascending pattern and is the following finger on the descending pattern.

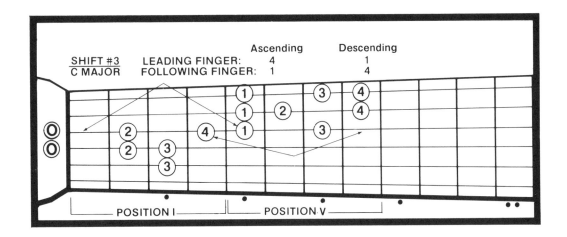

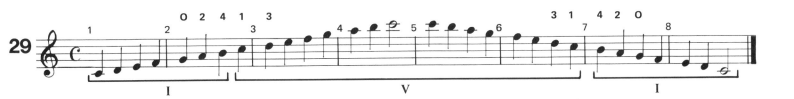

This exercise will help you develop your ability to shift positions. Practice slowly and carefully at first. After you have the finger patterns learned, you can increase the tempo.

SHIFTY

30

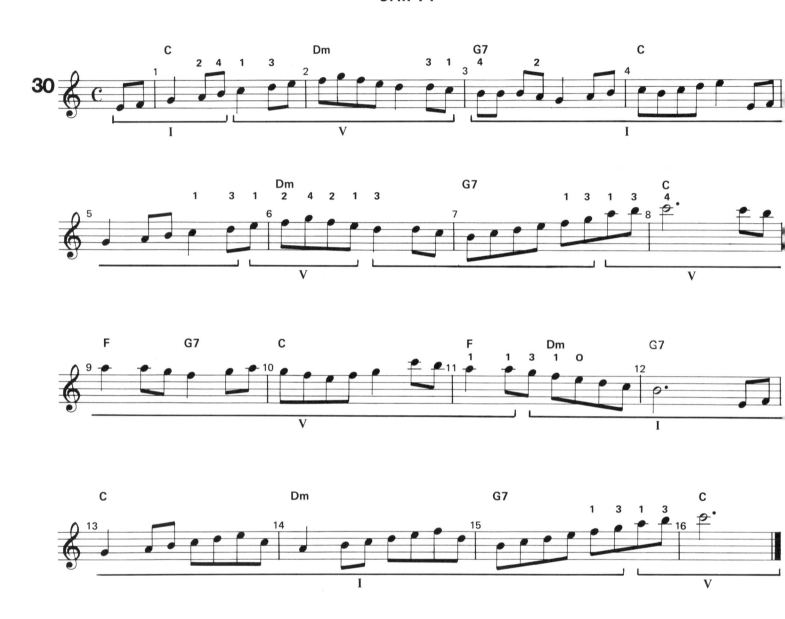

Finger Picking

The most flexible guitarist is the person who eventually learns to use a variety of right-hand techniques. One of these styles is to use the fingers rather than the pick for the right-hand playing. This can be utilized in blues, jazz, folk, popular, country, and classical music.

In this style the fingers are named with particular letters. The internationally accepted system is with the letters p, i, m, a. The illustration below shows how the fingers are denoted.

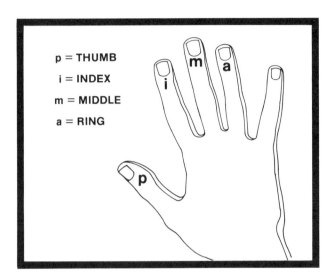

These general rules will help you as you begin learning this technique.

1. The thumb (p) plucks strings 4, 5, or 6 depending upon which string is the **root** of the chord. This motion is a downward stroke. Use the left side of the thumb followed by the thumbnail.

2. The other fingers (i, m, a) pluck the string in an upward stroke with the fleshy tip of the finger. As you complete the stroke, the fingernail will also contact the string. This is called a **free stroke** in classical technique.

3. The index finger (i) always plucks string 3.

4. The middle finger (m) always plucks string 2.

5. The ring finger (a) always plucks string 1.

6. The little finger is not used at first.

7. The thumb and each finger must pluck only one string per stroke and not brush over several strings. (This would be a strum.)

8. Let the strings ring throughout the duration of the chord.

Practice these arpeggios (broken chords) using the p-i-m-a pick.

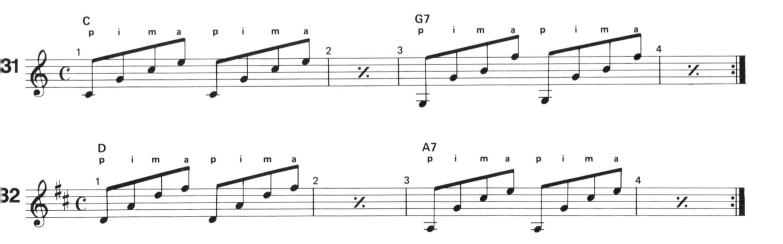

Practice the p-i-m-a picking pattern as an accompaniment for the following melodies. When the fingernails pluck the string, it should be a natural part of the pluck. Don't let the nails hook the strings and snap them against the fingerboard.

HE'S GOT THE WHOLE WORLD IN HIS HANDS

Always play with a full, even sound. Practicing too softly will not allow you to develop the best technique.

ROCK-A-MY SOUL

Be sure to learn the melody well before you play the accompanying part.

MAN OF CONSTANT SORROW

I am a man of con-stant sor-row, And I've seen trou - bles all my days. I'll bid fare - well to Minn-e-so-ta, The state where I was born and raised.

Continue picking
if going to next verse

2. All through this world I'm bound to ramble,
   Through sun and wind and drivin' rain,
   I'm bound to ride the Northern Railway.
   Perhaps I'll take the very next train.

Moving Chords Up The Neck

Any chord that is played in Position I can be moved up the neck. Any open strings in the original chord must also be moved up by replacing the nut of the guitar with a single finger or a **bar** (sometimes spelled **barre**). A bar is formed by placing the first finger across the strings needed for the chord. You can determine these new fingerings if you follow these rules:

1. Begin with a basic first position chord.

2. Keep the fingers in the same position as you move the chord up the neck.

3. Play a bar or single finger to replace the open strings of the original chord.

4. Find the name of the chord by counting up the frets. Be sure to count each fret as one half-step. For example, a C chord moved to the fifth fret (5 half-steps) would sound as an F chord. The quality of the chord (major, minor, or seventh) remains the same.

Moving The 3-String C Chord

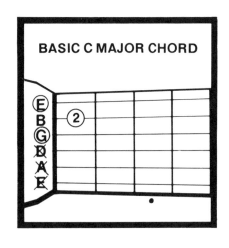

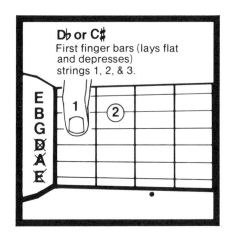

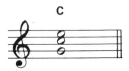

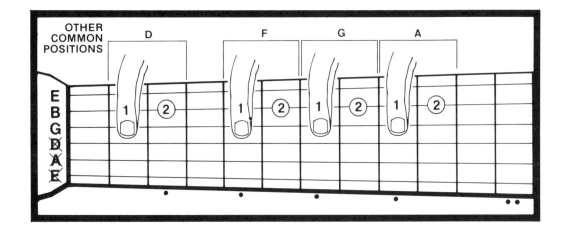

Study the fingering for the three-string A chord.

Moving The 3-String A Chord

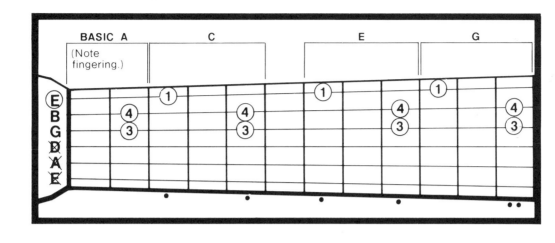

Can you move the 3-string A chord to a position that sounds the D chord?
(Answer: 1st finger in the fifth fret.)

Moving The 3-String G Chord

Be sure to look at the fingering for the chords before you begin to play them.

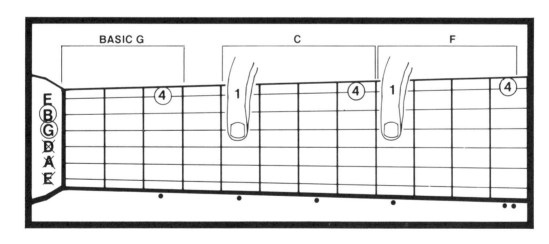

Can you move the 3-string G chord to a position that sounds the A chord?
(Answer: 1st finger bar in the second fret.)

Can you move the 3-string G chord to a position that sounds the D chord?
(Answer: 1st finger bar in the seventh fret.)

Moving The 3-String G7 Chord

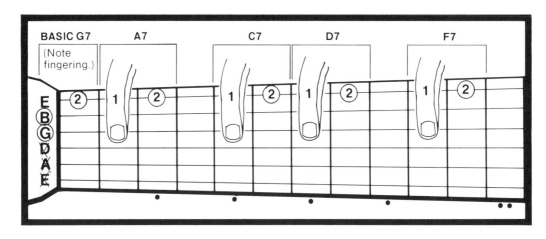

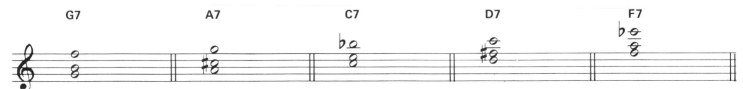

Can you move the 3-string G7 chord to a position that sounds B7?
(Answer: 1st finger bar in the fourth fret.)

Can you move the 3-string G7 chord to a position that sounds E♭7?
(Answer: 1st finger bar in the eighth fret.)

Moving The 3-String Dm Chord

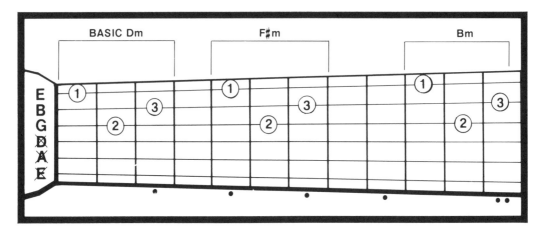

Can you move the 3-string Dm chord to a position that sounds:

Em? (Answer: 1st finger in the third fret.)

Gm? (Answer: 1st finger in the sixth fret.)

Am? (Answer: 1st finger in the eighth fret.)

24

Moving The E Chord

4 STRINGS AND 6 STRINGS

Study the four-string E chord finger positions before playing the chord.

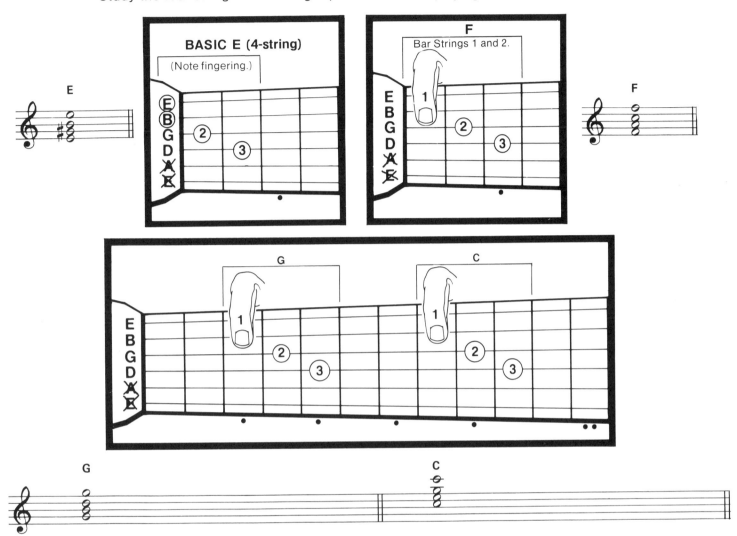

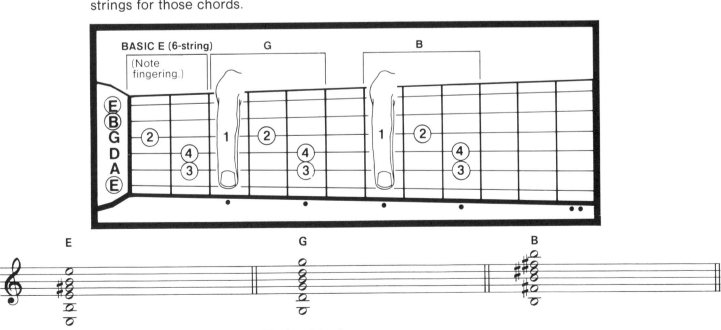

Can you move the basic E chord to sound: A? (Answer: 1st finger in the fifth fret.)

Any of the chords above can be played as three-string chords. Use the top three strings for those chords.

Can you move the 6-string E chord to form:

F? (Answer: 1st finger bar in the first fret.)

A? (Answer: 1st finger bar in the fifth fret.)

25

Moving The Am Chord

4 STRINGS AND 6 STRINGS

These four-string versions of the Am chord can also be played as three-string chords. Check the finger positions carefully before playing the chord.

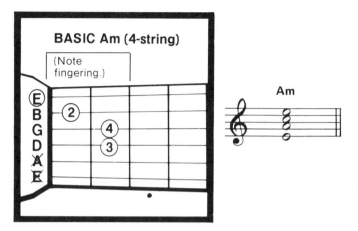

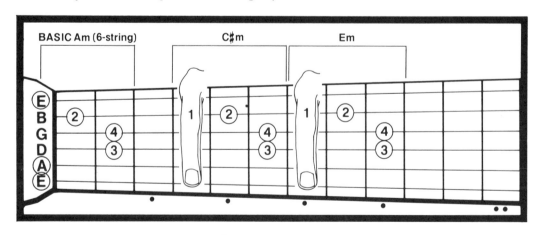

Can you find Cm? (Answer: 1st finger in the third fret.)

Now study the six-string Am chord finger positions.

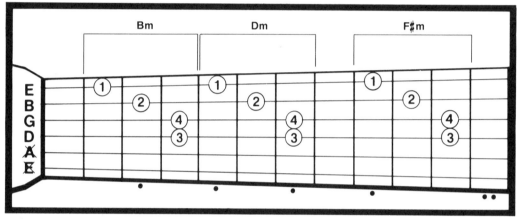

Can you find Bm? (Answer: 1st finger bar in the second fret.)

26

Other Moveable Chords

Remember to follow the same rules for moving the chords up the neck. Pay special attention to the fingerings because they may be somewhat different than those you know.

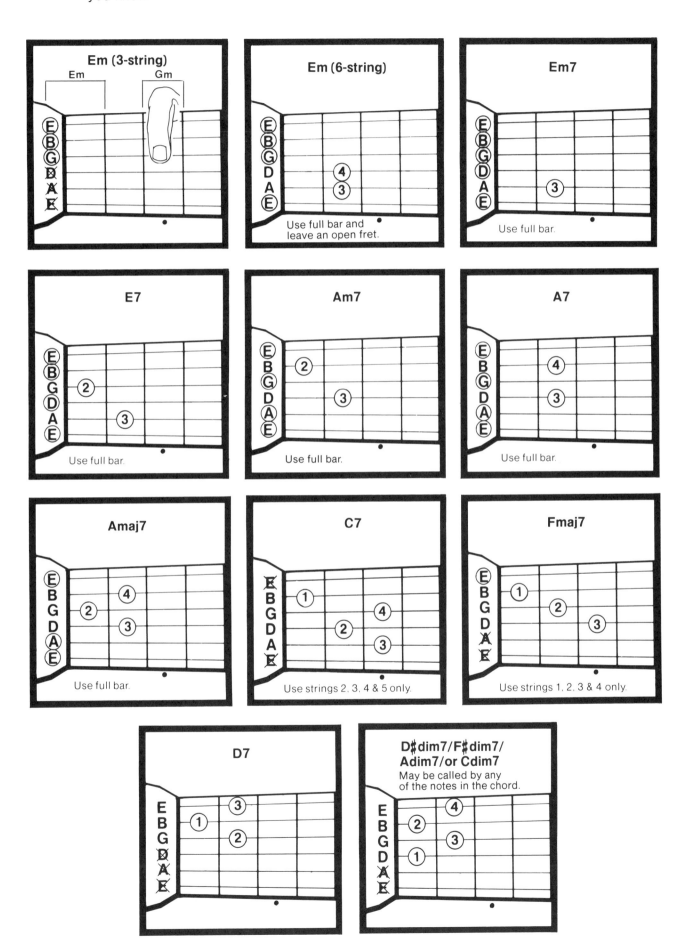

Em (3-string)

Em (6-string)
Use full bar and leave an open fret.

Em7
Use full bar.

E7
Use full bar.

Am7
Use full bar.

A7
Use full bar.

Amaj7
Use full bar.

C7
Use strings 2, 3, 4 & 5 only.

Fmaj7
Use strings 1, 2, 3 & 4 only.

D7

D♯dim7/F♯dim7/Adim7/or Cdim7
May be called by any of the notes in the chord.

Position V—F Major

The fingering pattern for the key of F in Position V is slightly different from the key of C. There is a B♭ in the key signature.

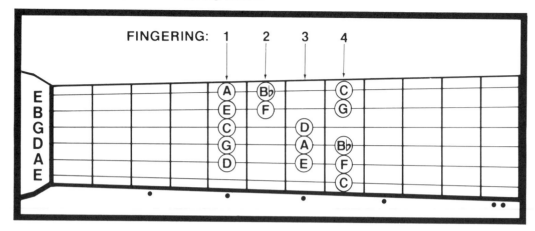

Play this exercise entirely in Position V.

First practice the melody for Exercise 37 in Position V. After you know the melody well, play the p-i-m-a-m-i picking pattern in the second part.

I SAW THREE SHIPS

Position IV—E Major

The E Major scale lies nicely in the fourth position. The fingering pattern will be the same as F Major in the fifth position. Practice the scale shown below.

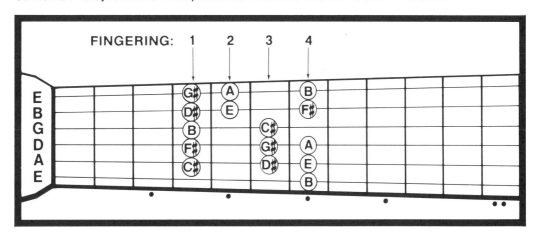

Learn the melody well before you play the chordal accompaniment. The melody should be played all in the fourth position. Remember to check the fingerings for the new chords and practice them alone.

HUSH, LITTLE BABY—JAZZ STYLE

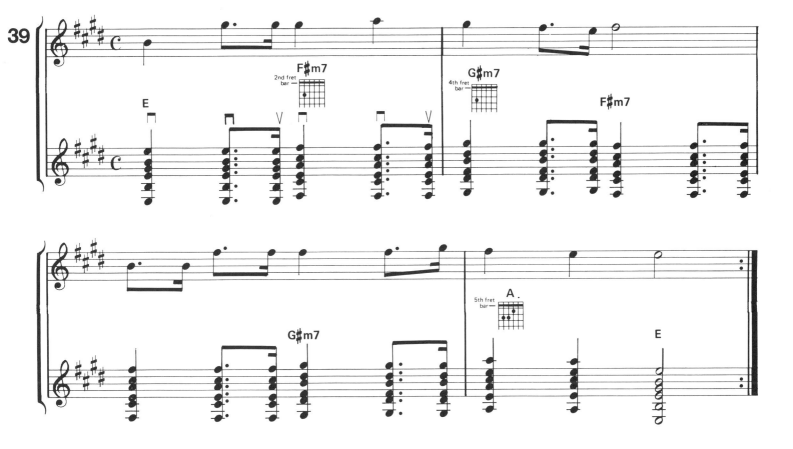

Position V—D Minor

Since D minor has the same key signature as F Major, you will be able to adapt easily to the fingerings you have just learned.

Remember that there is more than one type of minor scale. In the D minor scale there can be a C or a C♯. The chart shows you the fingering for both of these notes. Be sure to shift positions when indicated in the music.

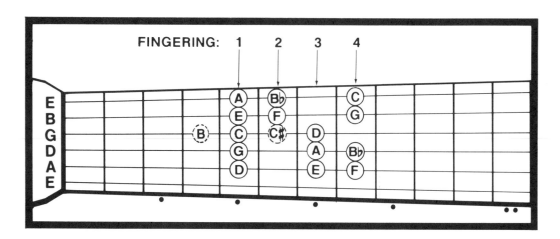

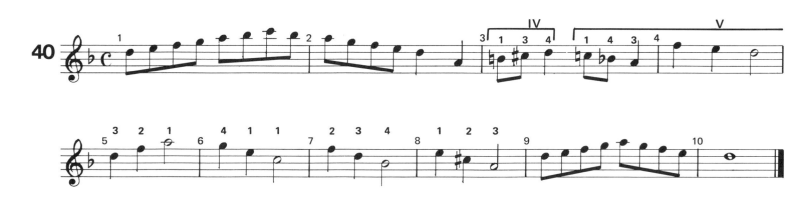

Practice the melody first in Position V. After you know the melody well, play the finger pattern shown in part 2.

GREENSLEEVES

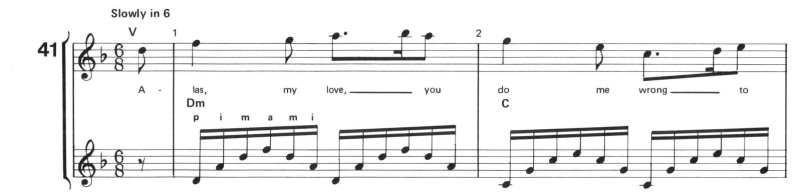

Bar Chord Blues/Rock

One of the best ways to learn to play bar chords up the neck is to practice the 12-bar blues with the chords shown below. The 12-bar blues became the basis for many of the rock and roll songs of the 1950's.

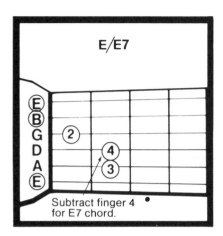

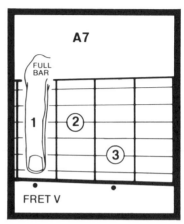

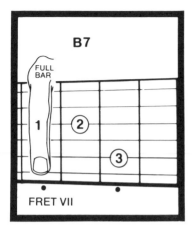

To play the bar chords A7 and B7 keep the fingers in the E7 formation and slide the hand up to the correct fret. The strumming rhythm shown is one that would sound good with this song.

SORE FINGER ROCK

Play Exercise 43 entirely with the E chord formation moved up and down the neck.
The G chord is barred at the third fret; the A chord at the fifth fret; and the B chord
at the seventh fret. If you need to check the finger position, look at page 25.

Remember to practice the melody before you play the strumming pattern.

HEY, GUITAR MAN

Triplets

Triplets are a way of subdividing a unit into three parts instead of two parts.

It will help if you think of playing in a $^6_8$ time signature. Remember that a moderate to fast $^6_8$ has two strong beats per measure. Exercises 44 and 45 should sound exactly the same.

Practice the following theme and variations on a familiar song, "Twinkle, Twinkle Little Star."

STARDOM VARIATIONS

Watch for the change in the time signature.

35

Studies In Thirds

One way to embellish the melody is to add a second part at the interval of a third above or below the melody. The technique of playing thirds is easy to do on a guitar by sliding the fingers up and down two adjacent strings. Study each of the fingering charts carefully; then play the exercises in thirds. Pay close attention to the fingerings given next to each set of notes.

C MAJOR—STRINGS 1 AND 2

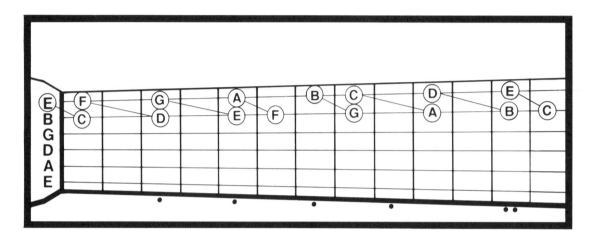

Notice that the finger combination 1 and 3 and the combination 1 and 2 come in pairs.

G MAJOR—STRINGS 2 AND 3

Now try thirds on strings 2 and 3.

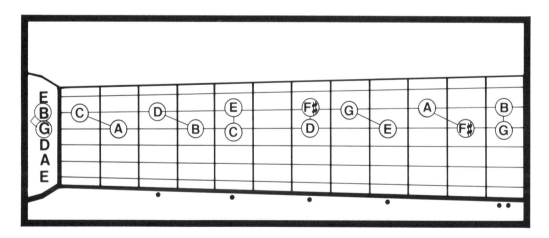

Notice that the finger combination 1 and 2 and the combination 2 and 3 come in pairs.

Practice the melody until you can play the thirds easily. After you know part 1 well, play the finger picking part. When fingers "a" and "m" are indicated in part 2, pluck both strings at the same time.

GOING LATIN

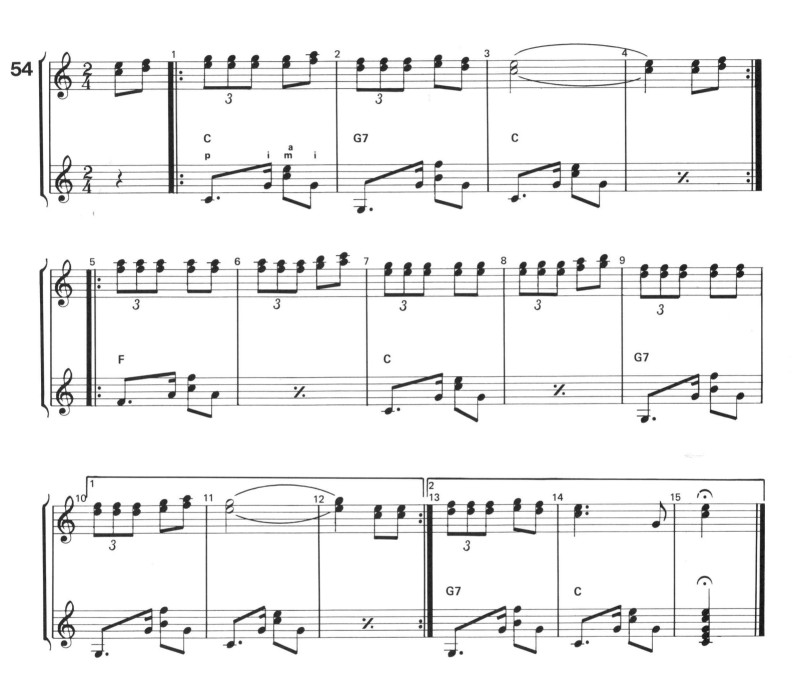

Now practice this song which has thirds on strings 2 and 3. If you have difficulty remembering the position, look at the chart on page 36.

In the second part watch the special position fingerings carefully in measures 1 and 9. These will make the part easier to play.

SHIFTING INTO THIRD

You may want to play this optional part in measure 4 (1st time only) or measure 8.

Remember to check all of the chord positions and fingerings before you begin to play a song. Any new chords will be shown in the music where the chord occurs.

ALL MY TRIALS

Practice the chorus slowly at first; later increase the speed so you don't slow down after the verse.

THE BRAZOS

Chorus (Melody is the lower note throughout the chorus.)

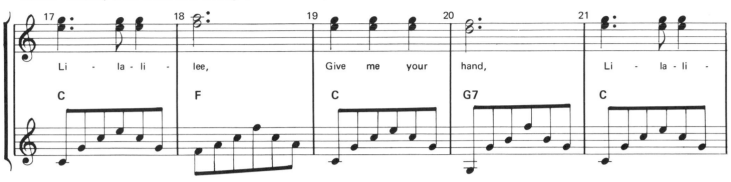

Li - la - li - lee, Give me your hand, Li - la - li -

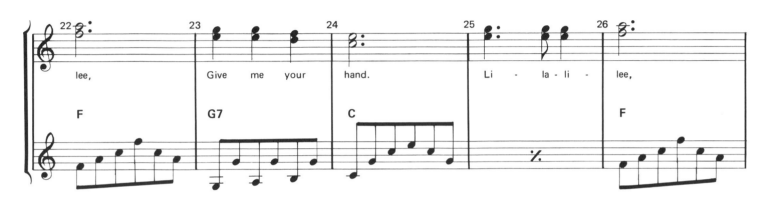

lee, Give me your hand. Li - la - li - lee,

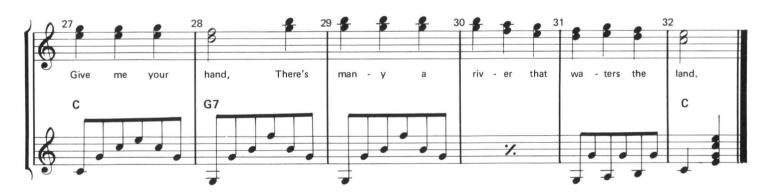

Give me your hand, There's man - y a riv - er that wa - ters the land.

2. The <u>sweet</u> Angelina runs <u>glo</u>ssy and <u>gli</u>ding,
   The <u>croo</u>ked Colo<u>ra</u>do runs <u>wea</u>ry and <u>wind</u>ing,
   The <u>slow</u> San Antonio it <u>cro</u>sses the <u>plain</u>,
   And I <u>ne</u>ver will <u>walk</u> by the <u>Bra</u>zos a<u>gain</u>.   CHORUS

3. She <u>hugg</u>ed me, she <u>kiss</u>ed me, she <u>called</u> me her <u>loved</u> one,
   The <u>Tri</u>nity's <u>mudd</u>y, but the <u>Bra</u>zos — quick<u>sand</u>y,
   She <u>hugg</u>ed me, she <u>kiss</u>ed me, she <u>called</u> me her <u>own</u>,
   And <u>down</u> by the <u>Bra</u>zos she <u>left</u> me a<u>lone</u>.   CHORUS

4. The <u>girls</u> of Little <u>Ri</u>ver, they're <u>plump</u> and they're <u>pre</u>tty,
   The <u>Sa</u>bine and the <u>Sul</u>phur have <u>ma</u>ny a beau<u>ty</u>,
   And <u>down</u> by the <u>Ne</u>ches there's <u>girls</u> by the <u>score</u>,
   And I <u>ne</u>ver will <u>walk</u> by the <u>Bra</u>zos no <u>more</u>.   CHORUS

Descending Bass Lines

Many guitar players use descending bass lines to add interest to their finger picking. These lines can be chromatic or they can be steps of a scale. Following is one example of a descending bass line. This line uses notes only on the fifth string.

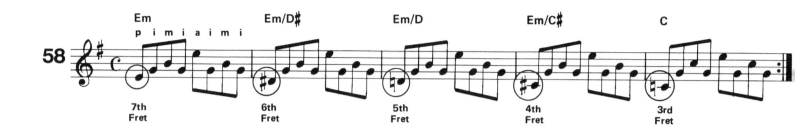

Be sure to practice the melody until you know it well before adding the finger picking part. Remember that you may have to change the rhythm of the melody to fit the words. The word on the first beat of whole note measure is underlined.

THE BUTCHER BOY

Her mother she went upstairs too, saying
"Daughter, oh what troubles you?"

2. "Oh mother, oh mother I cannot tell,
   That butcher boy I love so well,
   He courted me my life away
   And now at home he will not stay."

3. "There is a place in London town,
   Where that butcher boy goes and sits down.
   He takes that strange girl on his knee
   And he tells to her what he won't tell me."

4. Her father he came up from work,
   Saying where's my daughter, she seems so hurt.
   He went upstairs to give her hope
   And found her hanging from a rope.

5. He took his knife and cut her down,
   And in her bosom these words he found:
   Go dig my grave both wide and deep
   Place a marble slab at my head and feet.
   And on my coffin a snow white dove
   To show the world that I died of love.

Now try this arrangement of the song "The Butcher Boy." Practice both parts until you can play them well. You may want to ask your teacher or a friend to play a duet with you. If you have a tape recorder, record one part and play the other with it.

THE BUTCHER BOY

Position VII—D Major

Now move to Position VII to play in the key of D Major. Use the same fingering pattern that you learned for the C Major scale in Position V.

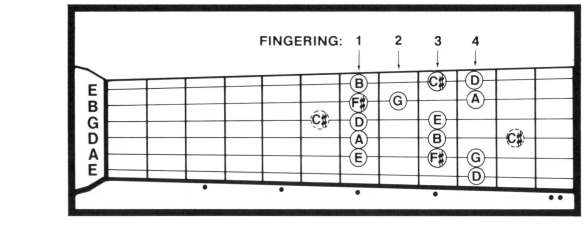

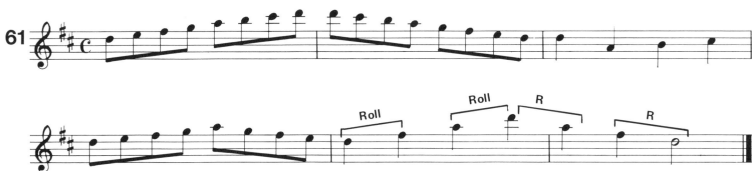

The following arrangement has three different parts. Learn the melody/chord line in part 2. After you can play it easily, practice the countermelody of part 1 in Position VII and finger picking style in part 3.

FLOW GENTLY, SWEET AFTON

Chord Chart

In this chart you will find all of the chords you learned in this book. There are also several of the more common chords you may see in other music you are playing. Remember that a string that is light grey should not be played.

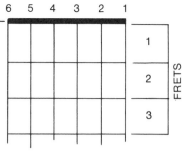

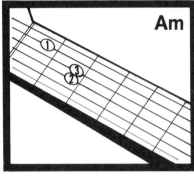 Am

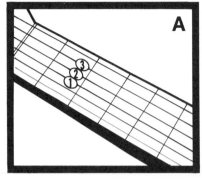 A

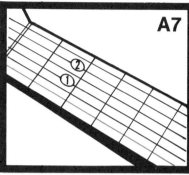 A7

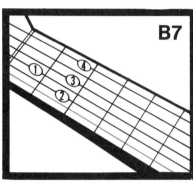 B7

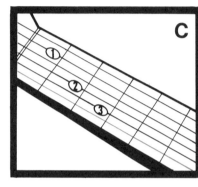 C

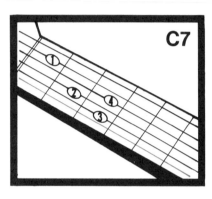 C7

 Dm

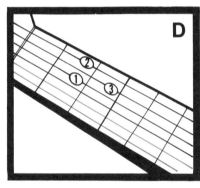 D

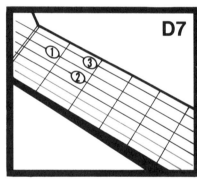 D7

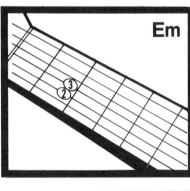 Em

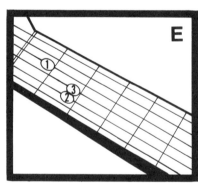 E

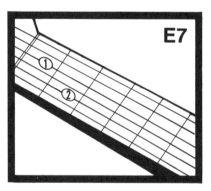 E7

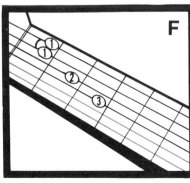 F

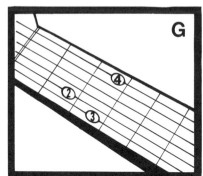 G

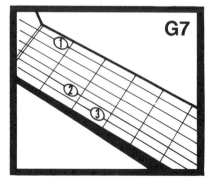 G7

Notes

THE HAL LEONARD GUITAR METHOD

MORE THAN A METHOD ...IT'S A SYSTEM.

This comprehensive method is preferred by teachers and students alike for many reasons:

- Learning Sequence is carefully paced with clear instructions that make it easy to learn
- Popular Songs increase the incentive to learn to play
- Versatile enough to be used as self-instruction or with a teacher
- Audio accompaniments let students have fun and sound great while practicing.

HAL LEONARD METHOD BOOK 1

Features great songs and provides beginning instruction which includes tuning, 1st position melody playing, chords, rhythms through eighth notes, solos and ensembles, and strumming. Also includes a handy chord chart. Pages are cross referenced for use with supplements.

00699010 Book...$4.95
00699026 Book/Cassette Pack $12.95
00699027 Book/CD Pack $14.95

HAL LEONARD METHOD BOOK 2

Book 2 includes studies and songs in the keys of C, G, D, Em, and F, syncopations and dotted rhythms, more advanced strums, the most common 1st position chords, solos, bass runs, and a variety of styles from bluegrass to blues-rock. A great selection of traditional songs, including "Simple Gifts," "Mamma Don't Low," "Roll In My Sweet Baby's Arms," "Jesu, Joy Of Man's Desiring," and many more. Pages are cross-referenced for supplements.
00699020 ....$4.95

HAL LEONARD METHOD BOOK 3

Book 3 includes the chromatic scale, 16th notes, playing in positions II-IV, moving chords up the neck (bar chords), finger picking, ensembles and solos, a wide variety of style studies and many excellent songs for playing and/or singing. Can be used with supplements.
00699030 ....$4.95

COMPOSITE

Books 1, 2 and 3 bound together in an easy-to-use comb binding.
00699040 ....$12.95

GUITAR METHOD SUPPLEMENTS

These unique books will work with *any* Guitar Method Books 1, 2, or 3. The play-along cassettes and CDs feature guitar on the left channel and full rhythm section on the right. Each book is filled with great pop songs!

EASY POP MELODIES

A unique pop supplement to any guitar method book 1. Cross-referenced with Book 1 pages for easy student and teacher use. Featured songs: Feelings • Let It Be • Every Breath You Take • You Needed Me • Heartbreak Hotel.

00699150 Book.............................$4.95
00699148 Book/Cassette Pack.....................$12.95
00697268 Book/CD Pack............................$14.95

MORE EASY POP MELODIES

A unique pop supplement to any guitar method book 2. Cross-referenced with pages for easy student and teacher use. Featured songs: Long And Winding Road • Say, Say, Say • King Of Pain • and more.

00699151 Book.............................$4.95
00699149 Book/Cassette Pack.....................$12.95
00697269 Book/CD Pack............................$14.95

POP MELODIES PLUS

Pop supplement cross-referenced to guitar book 3. Features: Cool Change • Daniel • Memory • Maneater • and many more.

00699154 Book.............................$4.95
00699156 Book/Cassette Pack...................$12.95
00699155 Cassette......................................$8.95
00697270 Book/CD Pack............................$14.95

FOR MORE INFORMATION, SEE YOUR LOCAL MUSIC DEALER, OR WRITE TO:

HAL•LEONARD CORPORATION
7777 W. BLUEMOUND RD. P.O. BOX 13819 MILWAUKEE, WI 53213

Prices, contents and availability subject to change without notice.

ROCK TRAX 1

This book is a supplement to ANY Method Book 1. It also teaches rhythm guitar, lead guitar and solo licks. The exciting play-along cassette features a great sounding rhythm section and demonstrates each exercise in the book. Rock Trax is unique because it provides the teacher with a program to teach rock guitar technique when the student begins lessons.
00699165 Book/Cassette Pack.....................$12.95
00697271 Book/CD Pack...........................$14.95

ROCK TRAX 2

This rock guitar supplement to any Method Book 2 teaches rhythm guitar, lead improvisation, and solo licks. The tape provides eight background rhythm tracks and demonstrates both the solo licks and new rock guitar techniques. Includes music and tablature.
00699167 Book/Cassette Pack.....................$12.95
00697272 Book CD/Pack............................$14.95

ROCK HITS FOR 1, 2 OR 3 GUITARS

Supplement to any Method Books 1 and 2. These arrangements are playable by 1, 2, or 3 guitars or class/ensemble. The tape features lead, harmony and rhythm guitar parts with band backup on Side A. Side B repeats the complete band accompaniments without guitar parts 1 or 2. "Practice Notes" aid the student and teacher with each song being ideal for lessons, recitals or at home enjoyment. Contents: Sister Christian • Rock Around The Clock • Johnny B. Goode • Rocket Man • Sad Songs (Say So Much) • Hungry Like The Wolf • Maggie May.
00699168 Book/Cassette Pack.....................$12.95
00697273 Book/CD Pack............................$14.95

INCREDIBLE CHORD FINDER

A complete guide diagramming over 1,000 guitar chords in their most common voicings. It is arranged chromatically and each chord is illustrated in three ways for three levels of difficulty. Note names of each string are indicated on each chord diagram to let the player know what notes are being played in the chord.
00697208 ....$5.95

BEGINNING GUITAR VIDEO

This video, especially cross-referenced with the Hal Leonard Guitar Method Book 1 and its supplements, Easy Pop Melodies and Rock Trax, teaches: • How to play chords • How to read music • How to play solos and duets • How to improvise rock • How to accompany any singing in wide variety of musical styles.
It's hosted by Will Schmid, one of the world's leading guitar teachers and authors, and features such great songs as "Every Breath You Take," "Mull Of Kintyre" and more. On-screen music, guitar diagrams, playing tips with close-up hand positions and demonstrations make for easy learning. Also includes Play-along Trax with full band accompaniment. 60 minutes.
00730627 ....$29.95